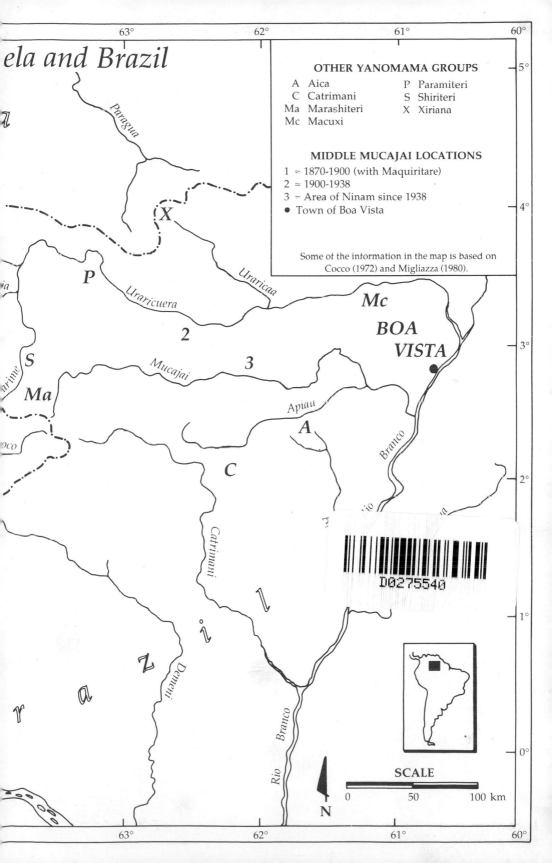

ela and Brazil

OTHER YANOMAMA GROUPS

A   Aica
C   Catrimani
Ma Marashiteri
Mc Macuxi

P   Paramiteri
S   Shiriteri
X   Xiriana

MIDDLE MUCAJAI LOCATIONS

1 ≈ 1870-1900 (with Maquiritare)
2 ≈ 1900-1938
3 ≈ Area of Ninam since 1938
● Town of Boa Vista

Some of the information in the map is based on
Cocco (1972) and Migliazza (1980).

BOA
VISTA

D0275540

SCALE

0   50   100 km

N

The Population Dynamics of the Mucajai Yanomama

The Population Dynamics of the Mucajai Yanomama

Canada

John D. Early

Department of Anthropology
Florida Atlantic University
Boca Raton, Florida

John F. Peters

Department of Sociology
Wilfrid Laurier University
Waterloo, Ontario
Canada

ACADEMIC PRESS, INC.
Harcourt Brace Jovanovich, Publishers
San Diego   New York   Berkeley   Boston
London   Sydney   Tokyo   Toronto

Photographs on p. ii and chapter opening pages courtesy of
Elmer Reiser, Steve Anderson, and John F. Peters.

Academic Press, Inc.
San Diego, California 92101

United Kingdom Edition published by
Academic Press Limited
24–28 Oval Road, London NW1 7DX

Library of Congress Cataloging-in-Publication Data

Early, John D.
  The population dynamics of the Mucajai Yanomama / John D. Early,
John F. Peters.
    p. cm.
  Includes bibliographical references.
  ISBN 0-12-227680-9 (alk. paper)
  1. Yanomama Indians--Social conditions. 2. Yanomama Indians-
-Population. 3. Mucajai River Valley (Brazil)--Social conditions.
4. Mucajai River Valley (Brazil)--Population. I. Peters, John F.
(John Fred), Date. II. Title.
F2520.1.Y3E27   1990
305.8'982082--dc20   89-17756
                                                         CIP

Printed in the United States of America
90 91 92 93   9 8 7 6 5 4 3 2 1

Contents

Illustrations

Tables

xi

Preface

This volume investigates the population dynamics of a group of Yanomama Indians, a foraging/horticultural group in northern Brazil, from
their first permanent contact with representatives of the "outer world"
in 1958 to 1987. The analysis employs the methods of quantitative
demography and qualitative ethnography. There have been few such
investigations of this type of population because of the problems of
obtaining complete and reliable data. To our knowledge, all previous
studies have been based on sketchy and/or very short-term data. These
required the questionable use of population models for their interpretation. The significance of this study is that it covers a 28-year time
span compiled from censuses, vital registries, genealogies, and ethnographic accounts drawn from the group itself. It gives insight into the
population dynamics not only of a postcontact situation, but also
allows some projections to be made of precontact conditions because
the permanent contact did not immediately cause a radical change of
all aspects of the precontact culture.

The book is conceived as a contribution to the population literature
of this type of small group, which is typical of the communities in
which humans lived for thousands of years. As such, it is also con-

ceived as a contribution to the study of the evolution of human population dynamics. The book is primarily addressed to anthropologists and evolutionary demographers. However anyone interested in population problems may find the material to be of interest.

Part One (the introduction) consists of three chapters which describe the Mucajai Yanomama, discuss the population dynamics of the precontact period, and give an overview of the 28-year postcontact period. In Part Two, each demographic variable (fertility, mortality, migration) is analyzed to understand its cultural antecedents as well as its magnitude and age–sex structure. Fertility is examined in Chapter Four, in-migration and out-migration in Chapter Six, and mortality in Chapter Seven. Chapter Five is a methodological chapter dealing with the problem of age estimation.

With each of the individual demographic variables and their cultural antecendents explained, there are two synthetic chapters comprising Part Three. Chapter Eight combines the information of the previous chapters and describes the interaction of the demographic variables with each other. It explains the change of size and age–sex structure of the Mucajai population in the postcontact period. Chapter Nine examines how the changed population structure has, in turn, affected the practice of some Yanomama cultural patterns. Part Four (Chapter Ten) concludes the analysis by comparing its results with those of other Yanomama groups. This allows extrapolation of the Mucajai material to the wider Yanomama area.

The authors wish to express their gratitude to various individuals and institutions who assisted the investigation. The following individuals read earlier versions of the manuscript and made invaluable suggestions: Dr. Michael Billig of Franklin and Marshall College, Dr. Francis Black of the Yale University School of Medicine, Dr. H. Dieter Heinen of the Instituto Venezuelano de Investigaciones Cientificas, Dr. Francis Johnston of the University of Pennsylvania, and Mrs. Lorraine Peters who was especially helpful with information about Yanomama women and health services. Dr. John Touhey of Florida Atlantic University greatly assisted in putting the manuscript into readable English. Dr. Laird Christie of Wilfrid Laurier University encouraged the project. Wilfrid Laurier University provided research and travel funds. The Mucajai missionaries of the Unevangelized Fields Mission provided hospitality as well as invaluable assistance by checking information with the Mucajai Yanomama. The pilots of the

Missionary Aviation Fellowship of North Brazil rendered logistical help. Mrs. Jacky Early provided hospitality for visitors passing through the Early household in conjunction with this project. Florida Atlantic University provided a personal computer and programs used in the analysis of the data and writing the manuscript.

John D. Early
John F. Peters

PART ONE

Introduction

One

The Mucajai Yanomama

This research is about a group of Yanomama Indians living on the Mucajai River (pronounced Mu-ká-sha-eé) in northern Brazil near the Venezuelan border. The term "Yanomama" (also spelled "Yanoama") is a generic designation for a group of indigenous people in Brazil and Venezuela who live in independent villages but who possess similar customs and languages. At present these groups live in an area approximately bounded by 0 to 5 degrees north latitude and 62 to 66 degrees west longitude.

Linguistically the Yanomama are subdivided into four languages (Migliazza, 1980): Sanema (Sanuma), Ninam (Yanam), Yanomam, and Yanomamo (Yanomamö, Yanomami, Yanomami). These language areas roughly correspond to the northern, southeastern, south central, and southwestern sectors of the Yanomama area (please refer to the map at the end of the volume). The southwestern group, the Yanomamo, are better known in the English-speaking world because of the Chagnon–Ashe films, the publications of Chagnon, and the translations of Lizot's works.

All these groups subsist by horticulture with plantains-bananas or manioc as the principle crop, by hunting forest animals, and by foraging for nuts, fruits, and honey. Each village is an autonomous unit organized by a cross-cousin kinship system with patrilineages. The lineages and affinal ties created by cross-cousin marriages are usually the strongest relationships (Chagnon, 1977; Lizot, 1984).

The number of Yanomama has been a topic of speculation for some time. Colchester (1985) estimates that there are about 21,000 Yanomama living in 363 villages: 11,752 Yanomamo in 171 villages, 5311 Yanomam in 64 villages, 3262 Sanema in 101 villages, and 856 Ninam in 27 villages. The 856 Ninam are scattered in three different areas: the northern group are 191 people living on the headwaters of the Paragua River in Venezuela and 226 on the Uraricaa River in Brazil; the central group are 355 people on the Mucajai and Apiau rivers, and the southern group are 81 people on the Ajarani River (please refer to the map at the beginning of the book) (Colchester, 1982). Although all these villages lie within the national boundaries of Venezuela or Brazil, most villages had little or no contact with the national societies until the last 10 years. For most villages sustained contact has been limited to missionaries, anthropologists, and medical technicians.

I. The Research Area

A group of Ninam (Yanam) Yanomama live on the middle Mucajai River in Brazil. This is on the eastern boundary of the Yanomama region at 3 degrees north latitude and 62 degrees west longitude (see map). In 1958 missionaries made the first permanent contact with this group and established a mission station near the two Ninam villages. By early 1987 there were 319 people living in six related villages. Two of these villages are less than an hour walk from the mission station. Two others are a 3-hour canoe trip upstream or west of the mission station and 15 minutes from each other. The remaining two are a 9-hour trip downstream or east of the mission station. For most purposes in this study, these six villages will be treated as a single unit. The social bases for doing so are their common origin and history, contemporary intermarriage, and relative isolation from other Yanomama and indigenous groups. The closest neighbors are the Marashiteri, who live a 4-day canoe trip to the west on the upper Mucajai. The Paramiteri live on the Uraricuera River, a 6-day trail and canoe trip to the northwest. The Aica live on the Apiau River, 5 days by trail to the southeast except for a small group who in more recent years have moved a day's journey to the east on the Mucajai. All these neighboring groups are Yanomama. The approximate locations of these groups are marked on the map.

The village is the focal point of social life. It consists of a single building which houses an entire group of 15 to 90 people. The villagehouse (yano) is a large, leaf-covered, cone-shaped dwelling 10–50 yards in diameter. The interior is completely enclosed by circular walls of leaves and a cone-shaped roof. It is dark except on the brightest days or when leaves of the sidewalls are pulled aside for lighting. The interior is usually hazy with smoke from many fires. Hammocks are strung from support poles near the walls of the house. The hammocks of each family are grouped around their fire, the focal point of family activity. Here food is cooked and eaten, babies are nursed, cotton is spun, and arrows are feathered. The large inner circle is primarily used for dancing and other festive activities.

The routine tasks are shifted out-of-doors in the late afternoon. A circle of packed earth 3–8 yards in width surrounds the building. Here the villagers squat or sit on a small slab of wood, perform tasks, and exchange experiences of the day or recount events from earlier times. Several trails extend from the house to nearby fields or to more distant hunting grounds.

Life is public both within and without the village-house. People know how one another's children behave and how a man treats his wife. They know what food others eat, what game a hunter captures, and what game was not successfully retrieved. Yanomama may respond to the activity of others with indifference, vocal anger, casual interest, or laughter.

Most activities begin at daybreak, around six in the morning. The long-range hunters rise first, eat bananas and cassava bread, and then make their exit for the day's hunt followed by a dog or two. Hunting is occasionally done individually, but usually in groups of two or three. Hunting companions are most often brothers or brothers-in-law. When fresh animal tracks are seen, the men form larger groups of 6 to 14 in anticipation of much game. The animals hunted are the macaw parrot, smaller parrot, toucan, partridge, trumpeter, bush chicken, bush turkey, spider monkey, howler monkey, capuchin monkey, wooly monkey, tapir, collared peccary, white-lipped peccary, capybara, paca, armadillo, agouti, and deer.

After the hunters depart, the rest of the villagers gradually awaken, leave the house to urinate and defecate, and return to squat near the fire for warmth. By eight o'clock everyone is working. Some men remain in the house to repair arrows or carve bows. Others may leave to hunt small game, work in their field, build a canoe, or fish. Sixteen varieties of fish are taken. Crops cultivated in the garden include bitter and sweet manioc, six types of bananas, two types of plantains, yams, sugar cane, peach palm fruit, red pepper, cotton, gourds, tobacco, and the bixa tree, which yields seeds used to make dye. The foods gathered in the jungle are three types of palm fruit, red berries, wild cashew fruit, brazil nuts, cacao, avocado, and honey. Some women will go to the fields for several hours to gather cassava roots and bananas while others remain in or near the house to spin cotton, process food, or care for children. Women work in the fields in groups of three to six, typically a mother with her daughters and daughters-in-law.

The men who fish or hunt small game do not go far and may return by three in the afternoon with a bird or several small fish. Between four and six o'clock the women with their wicker baskets and axes leave to chop firewood from logs gathered in the nearby jungle. The firewood is used to cook the evening meal and to supply warmth during the cool nights. The hunters who left early in the morning return about five or six in the evening. Their wives immediately cut the meat and cook it in a pot over the fire. The hunter lies in his hammock and is served bananas and cassava bread by his wife, daughter, or sister.

At dusk there is a general buzz of activity in the communal house. The women distribute the cooked meat according to their kinship-reciprocity obligations. Hunters do not eat the meat they brought, but receive meat from other hunters through the reciprocity network. The meat is eaten along with a piece of cassava bread. Animated conversation takes place during the evening meal and for at least 2 hours afterward. Then all retire for the night.

At the time of contact, the Mucajai group lived in two villages. Both were close to the Mucajai river but separated by a 7-hour trail or canoe trip. After the mission station was built near the river, the more distant village moved downstream to be closer to the missionaries. The villages have physically relocated a number of times, but the distance of each move is short. Moves are determined by the physical condition of the village-house, proximity to new fields, water supply, and availability of game. Village fission has also occurred as the two original villages have grown to six. It is a response to village size, marriages, and the desire to be either close to friendly families or distant from hostile ones. The fissioning of Mucajai villages has been relatively free of explosive tensions. Since contact, there has never been protracted violence within the group, although fist duels and heated verbal disputes have been frequent. In the early 1980s a group fissioned and established a new village about 7 hours downstream, a considerable move away from the other Mucajai groups. In the middle 1980s this group fissioned again. The majority moved further downstream to help construct and then live near an airstrip established by FUNAI (the Indian Agency of the Brazilian government). Both downstream groups have decreased their contacts with the other Mucajai groups and the mission. It is the initiation of a distinct community centered on the FUNAI airstrip. For the purposes of this study, these downstream groups are considered part of the Mucajai group since most of their postcontact history occurred as members of this group.

II. The First Permanent Contact

When missionaries made aerial surveys in 1955, they noted the location of the Yanomama villages in the Roraima area. Fish hooks were dropped from the survey plane as a gesture of good will. In 1956 a group of Mucajai men traveled overland in a southeasterly direction to find Brazilians and obtain steel goods. They saw indications that Brazilians had been in the area, but failed to make any contact. In 1957 and 1958 trips downstream on the river were made for the same reason and were successful. In November 1958 John Peters and Neill Hawkins, representing the Unevangelized Fields Mission, made the first permanent contact with the Mucajai Yanomama. In the previous September, missionaries had flown over both the Aica on the Apiau River and the larger Mucajai village. The Aica chief drew an arrow in order to shoot the plane, probably due to previous hostile contacts with Brazilian rubber cutters. No hostility was shown by the Mucajai group. Gifts of metal knives, fish hooks, beads, and a few scissors were dropped from the plane to secure their good will. The Mucajai people indicated their friendliness by raising a banana stalk in the air as a gift to the people in the plane. The missionaries returned to their base on the Guiana–Brazilian border. They enlisted the aid of two Waiwai Indians to accompany them up the Mucajai. On the lower reaches of the river, they passed Brazilians who described the Mucajai Ninam as fierce killers with bows and arrows taller than any man. (Since the missionaries did not return by river, the Brazilians assumed they had been killed.) Peters later described the first encounter in these words.

There was no one in the area when we arrived by canoe after four-teen days of travel up the river. We stood in the river holding a ma-chete, offering it to our unseen hosts. I heard (erroneously) leaves rus-tling and thought someone was taking aim at us with arrows. I was scared and did not know if we would come out of this alive. For two nights we camped on an island, feeling more secure there than if we were on the mainland. Still no one appeared. We summoned up our courage and walked into their large village (yano). It was empty. The Waiwai said the Mucajai people had been there within the past week. Cautiously we walked up a trail for about two hours and saw further signs of their presence.

The villagers arrived the next day. They had been having a feast at an intermittently used village. They were enthusiastic and overjoyed. We gave a machete as a gift to a man who appeared to be the leader. The Mucajai people were attracted by the beads worn by the Waiwais. Several took the beads from the Waiwais and put them on themselves. In the confusion some were not returned and we wondered what it meant and what should be done about it.

We knew only three or four Waica words, so most of our communica-tion was done by demonstration. We identified ourselves by a painted model of the missionary airplane. We indicated with help of the model that it wished to land and that it needed a long field. They were de-lighted and willingly helped in cutting trees and leveling the ground. After a week of work, we paid them with steel goods which were enthu-siastically received. These activities established friendship. About a week after this the plane came and dropped food, trade goods and mail. Apparently a bundle of machetes was also dropped, but was snatched and hidden before seen by any of the missionaries. This was not discov-ered until sometime later. The Mucajai people were delighted with the presence of people with an eternal source of steel goods. Shortly after-ward my leg was severely injured by a falling tree and we almost gave up the mission effort.

A small mission station was established within a short distance of one of the villages. Peters lived at the mission station beginning in

1958 and was joined by his new bride in 1959. They and their growing family remained until February 1967 with the exception of a year in Canada in 1962–63. Peters also lived in the village-house in order to learn the language, to understand the daily life, and to participate in hunting expeditions. He was incorporated into the kinship system by being made an adopted brother of a friend. In this way he acquired a kinship status to all in the group which enabled him to interact as a recognized member of the community.

Upon his return from Brazil, Peters obtained a doctorate in social science. While writing his dissertation, he returned to the area in 1972 as an investigator. Peters' change of roles was explained to the Yanomama but not well understood. On his return visits, Peters engaged in no missionary activity and concentrated his efforts on furthering his knowledge of the culture. He returned again in 1979 and 1987 to do further research. Peters (1974, 1975, 1980, 1982, 1984, 1987) has published ethnographic accounts of different aspects of the culture.

In the 1980s gold was found in the region of the Mucajai Yanomama. This has increased their contact with the national society, and in the past few years visits to the district capital, Boa Vista, have become routine. Cultural changes have also begun, changes which will accelerate in the next few years. In mid-1987, armed violence erupted between the Yanomama and Brazilian mining prospectors who had entered their traditional hunting grounds. Three Marashiteri, one Mucajai, and five Brazilian miners were killed. In 1988 as the final version of this manuscript is being written, an estimated 20,000 Brazilian miners are streaming up the Mucajai River. The Brazilian government has asked the missionaries to leave the area. The Mucajai River has become polluted. The future of the Yanomama and their homeland is threatened.

III. Purpose of the Research

This research examines the population dynamics of the Mucajai Yanomama. The demographic dynamics of a population are the net result of fertility, mortality, in-migration, out-migration, and the resulting age–sex structure of the population. These demographic variables are influenced by many aspects of Yanomama culture and they, in turn, affect the culture. This interaction of cultural and demographic variables defines the population dynamics of a group.

The investigators believe that this is the most comprehensive population study to date of a Yanomama group. These groups are considered one of the last examples of the human condition in a setting of small-scale societies. There have been previous attempts to understand the demographic structure and population dynamics of these groups but, as will be discussed in Chapter 10, these efforts have been frustrated by inadequate data and/or the use of unsatisfactory estimation procedures. The significance of this study is its foundation on a reliable demographic–ethnographic database yielding both qualitative and quantitative data for a time span of 30 years.

IV. Sources of the Mucajai Database

The database contains information about 551 individual Yanomama drawn from several sources. Since the analysis is dependent on the accuracy of these data, it is important to examine the quality of each source. The first concern is the completeness of the enumeration of individuals, e.g., a census, birth, or death register. Then there is the question of the accuracy of the information about personal characteristics such as sex, age, and relationships of family members. The enumeration of age in nonliterate populations is especially difficult and will be treated separately in Chapter 5.

A. Censuses, 1972 and 1979: Name, Sex, Age by Family Groups

Peters compiled censuses in 1972 and 1979 each reporting the above-mentioned variables. Because of his experience and kinship status in the community, there were no difficulties. He was able to cross check and clarify any ambiguities from his personal knowledge of the people or by verbal interrogation.

B. Birth Registration, 1958–1986: Name, Sex, Date of Birth, Names of Parents

The missionaries have maintained a register of births since contact. At least every few months the mission station saw each member of the group except from the mid-1980s, when the downstream groups separated. Mission personnel had an interest in births, observed pregnancies, and visited mothers in the postnatal period. (Mrs. Lorraine Peters is a registered nurse.) In return visits Peters has repeatedly verified the birth registers and has never found any surviving person whom they omitted.

C. Death Registration, 1958–1986: Name, Sex, Age at Death, Apparent Cause

The missionaries also maintained a register of deaths. Most deaths came to their immediate attention. When infants became ill, the missionaries were frequently summoned to the village-house or the infant brought to the mission station. If a pregnant mother was later seen without a nursing child, inquiry would be made. The missionaries knew every individual and if he or she had not been heard from or recently seen, questions would be asked. On return trips Peters verified and updated the accuracy of the death register. It missed a few infanticides to be discussed later and there was one case of mistaken identification. These problems occurred when regular mission personnel were temporarily absent from the mission. The death register allowed the inclusion in the database of all individuals living in the group at the time of contact but who died before the first census.

D. Genealogies

Genealogies were constructed for family groups going back at least two generations before contact.

E. The Quantitative Database

From these sources a database of 551 persons was assembled. For each individual a record was coded and computerized consisting of the following variables: ID number, name, sex, date of birth, source of birth date, date of in-migration (if applicable), reason for in-migration, group from which in-migrated, date of out-migration, reason for out-migration, date of death, source of death date, cause of death, ID number of mother, ID numbers of recognized fathers, and villages of residence in 1955, 1958, 1974, 1980, and 1986.

Of the 551 people in the database, only 463 lived in the Mucajai group between 1959 and 1987. The remainder are ancestors of these people who died before the contact period or relatives of in-migrants to the Mucajai group who did not enter the group themselves. Every record in the database was subjected to intense scrutiny by the investigators. Consistency checks were made from genealogical, demographic, and ethnographic viewpoints to ensure their accuracy. Problems were clarified by letters to the missionaries and by Peters' visit in early 1987.

Sixty percent of the birth dates were recorded by registration and pose no problem. The remaining 40% were derived by estimation. Since the methodology of estimation relies upon the biological clock underlying the reproductive period, the procedure is explained after discussion of the reproductive period in Chapter 4. With the dates of birth, death, in-migration, and out-migration established, a population register for each of the 28 postcontact years was developed. The register for each year contained the records of all individuals who lived in the population that year.

F. The Qualitative Database: The Ethnographic File

Another source of data is the ethnographic information compiled by Peters during his 8 years of residence among the Mucajai Yanomama and that collected during his return visits in 1972, 1979, and 1987. This will be used in conjunction with quantitative data to describe the reciprocal influence between the cultural and demographic variables. A methodological tenet of this study is that explanatory power follows from a judicious combination of both quantitative and qualitative data.

V. Some Editorial Considerations

The presentation of the research presumes readers from two disciplines: demography and cultural anthropology. This has posed some problems because there has been limited interaction between these groups. Some demographic indices and conventions are briefly explained for anthropologists who may not be familiar with them. Conversely, some details of ethnographic and genealogical work have been briefly explained for demographers. Readers unfamiliar with the Yanomama might find it helpful to peruse Lizot's (1988) or Cocco's (1972) presentation in Spanish of Yanomama history and ethnology. In English, there is Chagnon's (1983) presentation. Cocco, Chagnon, and Lizot worked in the southwestern region of the Yanomama, which has some ethnographic differences from the Ninam region of the Mucajai Yanomama.

The Yanomama have been the focus of controversies in contemporary anthropology. This research presents the population dynamics of the group without direct reference to these disputes. While the authors believe this book is pertinent to the debates, our goal is the presentation of the population dynamics within a demographic–anthropological framework. To discuss the disputes would have skewed the presentation and obstructed the primary task.

Two

The Population Dynamics of the Precontact Period

The interpretation of the population dynamics in the postcontact period requires some knowledge of precontact times and the population found at the time of the first permanent contact in 1958. This historical context is the topic of this chapter.

I. History of the Yanomama

Migliazza (1982), employing a methodology of evolutionary linguistics, sees the ancestors of the contemporary Yanomama arriving from the north to a place on the upper Ucayali River in Peru about 4000 B.P. (before the present). This was a group of proto-Pano-Tacanan speakers. Around 2600 B.P., proto-Panoan speakers from this group moved to the lower Ucayali and west into what is now Brazil. Here speakers of proto-Yanomama separated around 2500 B.P., traveled down the Amazon river and up the Rio Negro, and settled near the confluence with the Rio Branco. From here they gradually spread out and occupied the area drained by the tributaries of the lower Rio Branco for over 1000 years. Around 1000 B.P. they began moving in waves toward the Parima Highlands and the headwaters of the Orinoco River. Lizot (1977) believes this movement was in part due to conflicts with the Arawaks and later with European slave traders.

Cocco (1972), who worked among the Yanomama for 15 years, has attempted to reconstruct their recent history from accounts of early contacts and the testimony of the Yanomamo themselves. He places the heartland of contemporary Yanomama culture in the Parima Highlands between the headwaters of the Orinoco, Orinoquito, Ocamo, Putaco, Parime, Inaja, Mucajai, and Catrimani rivers (see map). Cocco believes the first out-migrations from this heartland took place about 200 years ago. The reasons are not clear. These migrations were in a northerly direction, along the mountains forming the watersheds of the rivers in the region. This direction was taken as the other directions were blocked by other indigenous groups, by jungles with heavy growth, or by rivers with impassable rapids.

The first waves of out-migrants began to meet other indigenous groups including the Maku and the Maquiritare (Yekwana, Mayongong). From them the Yanomama adopted such things as the loincloth, manioc, fishing, river navigation, and canoe building. They lost their ethnocentric fierceness and began to intermarry with these groups. Linguistic evolution also took place. Today these groups are known as the Sanema. (Based on linguistic evidence, Migliazza places this out-migration earlier than Cocco's estimate. He thinks the Sanema language evolved about 600 years ago.)

Toward the end of the last century another wave of out-migration took place. This migration also started in a northerly direction but then swung east along the Pacaraima Range and the Uraricuera River. This group also met Maku and Maquiritare groups and from them learned how to build canoes. Within the group, fissioning took place. Subgroups migrated northeast and eventually reached the streams forming the headwaters of the Paragua and Uraricaa rivers on the Brazilian–Venezuelan border. Other groups went south to the the the Mucajai and Apiau rivers. Language evolution took place. Today these are the Ninam (Yanam) Yanomama groups and this research examines the group on the middle Mucajai River.

In this century a third wave of out-migration from the Parima Highlands took place toward the southeast and southwest. Those who went toward the southeast comprise the current Yanomama settlements on the Ajarani, Catrimani, and Demeni rivers. Those who went toward the southwest have reached the area drained by the Mavaca, Siapa, Cauaburi, Marauia, Marari, and Lower Orinoco rivers. The exodus in this century seems to have been caused by heavy fighting between Yanomama villages.

II. The Mucajai Yanomama

This research examines a Ninam Yanomama group on the middle Mucajai River. The following account has been derived from ethnohistorical work with the Mucajai people supplemented by Chagnon's (Chagnon et al., 1970; Chagnon, 1972) survey of the Ninam area. Between 1870 and the turn of the century the ancestors of the contemporary Mucajai and other Ninam groups were living on the south bank of the Auaris River in a village adjacent to or also occupied by a Maquiritare (Yekwana) group (see map). There was some intermarriage. Continual seduction of Ninam women by the Maquiritare led to conflict and the Ninam Yanomama left the village. They moved eastward, downstream, and settled on the south bank of the Uraricuera River.

At this new location several events occurred whose chronology is not certain. Around 1900 two females were taken captive by the Ninam in raids on the Wehe peoples. These were the mothers of two older women whom Peters met in the Mucajai group at the time of their contact with the missionaries. Several women in-migrated for marriage from the Wehe and another unknown group. There was conflict with the Macuxi, who stole a Ninam woman. In revenge the Ninam Yanomama raided the Macuxi and killed one of their men. During this period, according to Chagnon, there was an epidemic of unknown origin which caused many male deaths. Sometime during residence on the Uraricuera River, conflict also arose within the Ninam group. Some left the village and moved east. Currently this is a separate Ninam group, the Xiriana, living on the Uraricaa River and the headwaters of the Paragua River.

Around 1936 a Maku family was returning upstream after trading with Brazilians. They were noticed by the Ninam, who lured them to the river bank under the pretext of wishing to exchange gifts. The

Ninam seized their trade goods, killed the husband and two sons, and took the wife captive. She was taken as wife by a Ninam and lived among the Mucajai group until her death in 1982.

Sometime during the 1930s the Maquiritare group, from whom the Ninam had originally separated, descended the Uraricuera and killed a Ninam Yanomama while he was gathering palm fruit. In retaliation, the Ninam raided the Maquiritare village, killed all the men, took their steel goods, and fled with four women captives. (Chagnon has a differing version of the beginning of this battle. The Maquiritare were looking for material to build canoes. A friendly visit with the Ninam quickly turned into a battle. The Ninam had blamed the epidemic on them and wanted revenge.) Whatever the reason for the original Ninam raid on the village, the Maquiritare raided the Ninam in retaliation. It is reported that many men were killed on both sides. Genealogical information indicates that at least five Ninam Yanomama men were slain. Also killed was one of the Maquiritare women who had been previously abducted by the Ninam.

During the 1930s the Ninam moved further south for protection against the Maquiritare. This brought them to creeks that eventually flowed into the Mucajai River. Additional moves took them south over the Mucajai, and then back north to creeks that flowed toward the Uraricuera, then south again to the Mucajai watershed, and finally to the present settlement area on the north bank of the Mucajai itself. They appear to have arrived there in the early 1950s. Since their last contact with the Maquiritare about 1938, they had been isolated from all other groups.

There were two distinct groups comprising what is called here "the Mucajai Yanomama." The largest was a group called, at the time of contact, the Borabuk, the people of the falls. The name comes from the rapids on the Mucajai near their village. The other was the Kaserapai, the people of the long lips. This latter group was first reported living in the vicinity of the Borabuk after the Maquiritare wars. According to Cocco (1972) the name "Kaerapais" was originally used by the Maku for all the Yanomama because of their habit of placing a large plug of tobacco between their lower lip and teeth. With time, it enlarges the lower lip. It appears that among the Mucajai group, the general term was later restricted to one village while the other took its name from the rapids near their village. In spite of occasional tensions, friendly relations prevailed between the groups. They usually moved and settled in the same general area. Nevertheless, there was little intermarriage between them. When both groups settled on the Mucajai, intermarriage began. One of the villages is still known as that of the Kaserapai, but it now contains both Kaserapai and Borabuk, as do almost all the villages designated here as "Mucajai Yanomama".

By around 1950 the Mucajai Yanomama were depleting their supply of steel tools obtained in previous raids. At this time teams from the Brazilian Boundary Commission were exploring the eastern watersheds of the Parima mountains in preparation for demarcating the international boundary with Venezuela. They left five machetes and an ax in a tree near the river as a goodwill gesture. They were found by the Ninam and this precipitated the move to banks of the Mucajai River, where they hoped to meet the people who made steel tools.

In 1955 fish hooks dropped from the missionaries' plane stimulated the Mucajai to attempt to make contact with the makers of steel goods. Some Mucajai men traveled overland in a southwesterly direction to the Apiau River where the Aica lived. They saw some Aica from a distance but had no interest in making contact. They were unsuccessful in locating any Brazilians, but saw indications that they were in the region. In October 1957 an all-male party journeyed down the river for the same purpose. This time they were successful. They received clothing and two or three used axes and knives from the Brazilians in return for canoes and many arrows. However no permanent contact resulted and the group immediately returned upstream to their village. In September 1958 another successful trading trip was made by a group that included some women. From these trips and an earlier aerial survey, the presence of the Mucajai Yanomama became known to the Brazilians of the Roraima Territory and to the missionaries.

III. Population Dynamics of the Precontact Period

A. The Problem

The Mucajai Yanomama state that during the precontact period they were a larger group than they were at the time of the first permanent contact. Given their rudimentary counting system, the exact decrease cannot be estimated. This section examines the components of population change in light of the fragmentary history to obtain some understanding of the population dynamics of this period.

B. Fertility

The Yanomama women say that they are bearing children in the same way and with the same frequency in the postcontact period as in the precontact period. The level of individual fertility (total fertility rate) derived in Chapter 4 is about eight live births. Table 2.1 shows that group fertility for 1955–1958 was low for a total fertility rate of eight. It was also low compared with the rates of the postcontact phases shown in Figure 4.2. The reason is indicated in Table 2.2. At the time of contact females comprised only 36.4% of the total population. More importantly, they comprised only 22.6% of the population between the ages of 15 and 44 (last column of table). This sexual imbalance produced relatively low group fertility for a community with a total fertility rate of about eight.

C. In-Migration

Isolation from other groups prevented in-migration during the 20 years prior to contact. The historical accounts indicate two sources of inmigration in the earlier precontact period, female captives seized in raids and women coming for marriage. At the time of contact 5 of the 44 females (11.6%) were seized women. This indicates that inmigration was a significant factor in the population dynamics before the period of isolation.

Table 2.1
Crude Birth, Death, and Natural Increase Rates per 1000 Population, 1955–1958 (Precontact)

Year	Birth	Death	Natural increase
1955	25.6	8.5	17.1
1956	33.5	8.4	25.1
1957	24.8	24.8	0.0
1958	8.3	25.0	− 16.7
Total	23.0	16.8	6.2

Table 2.2
Age and Sex Distribution, November, 1958 (Contact)

Age	Male	Female	Total	% Total	% Female	% Female
0	3	7	10	8.3	70.0	
5	8	6	14	11.6	42.9	
10	8	5	13	10.7	38.5	48.6
15	7	6	13	10.7	46.2	
20	10	1	11	9.1	9.1	
25	8	1	9	7.4	11.1	
30	12	4	16	13.2	25.0	
35	6	2	8	6.6	25.0	
40	5	0	5	4.1	0.0	22.6
45	3	2	5	4.1	40.0	
50	4	4	8	6.6	50.0	
55	1	1	2	1.7	50.0	
60	1	3	4	3.3	75.0	
65	0	1	1	.1	100.0	
70+	1	1	2	1.7	50.0	54.5
Total	77	44	121	100	36.4	36.4
Median age	27.2	18.2	24.6			
Borabuk						
0–14	16	15	31	36.5	48.4	
15–44	28	10	38	44.7	26.3	
45+	8	8	16	18.8	50.0	
Total	52	33	85	100	38.8	
Kaserapai						
0–14	3	3	6	16.7	50.0	
15–44	20	4	24	66.7	16.7	
45+	2	4	6	16.7	66.7	
Total	25	11	36	100	30.6	

D. Mortality

Table 2.1 shows the crude death rates for the 4 years immediately preceding permanent contact. The 2 years of low mortality are consistent with similar years in the postcontact period shown in Figure 7.1. The 2 years of high mortality are primarily due to the impact of infectious disease contracted on the downstream trips. This high-mortality period indicates that there may have been heavy mortality in precontact times due to infectious disease carried from the rural Brazilian or Venezuelan populations by third parties such as the Maquiritare and

Macuxi. Chagnon mentions an incidence of infectious disease among the Mucajai group, although the fact that it seems to have killed only males raises some doubts. Five males are known to have died in the raids by the Maquiritare. This appears to be high mortality given the probable size of the group at that time. Isolation during the 20 years before contact would have prevented mortality due to raids and infectious disease.

Another mortality factor discussed in the Yanomama literature is preferential female infanticide. Although infanticide involves both sexes, there are occasions when an infant is killed because it is female. This practice could have a devastating impact on the size of a population. It not only elevates mortality, but by its sex preference it lowers future group fertility. The important question here is whether this custom was practiced frequently enough so that it became a significant factor in precontact population decrease. Because of the sketchy data for the precontact period, this is among the most difficult of the analytical questions of this research. Information from the postcontact period can assist with its analysis. Consequently discussion of the role of preferential female infanticide in the precontact period is postponed to the last chapter.

E. Out-Migration

The ethnohistorical information indicates fissioning as an important source of out-migration. The community currently known as the Xiriana was originally part of the Mucajai group. There is no indication of how many people left, but it is known that sizable numbers can leave Yanomama villages when fissioning occurs. Once again, the 20-year isolation moderated the possible impact of fissioning. Another out-migration factor is Mucajai women seized in raids by other groups. Two women are known to have been taken, but there may have been more.

F. Population Decrease

What was the reason for the precontact population decrease? It is difficult to assign any specific cause. The forces of population increase, namely the group levels of fertility and in-migration, were held to moderate levels by sexual imbalance and the 20 years of isolation. The forces of decrease, mortality and out-migration, were likewise moderated by the isolation. There were heavy mortality losses immediately before contact because of infectious diseases contracted during the downstream trips. These alone could account for the diminished numbers mentioned by the Yanomama after contact. The factors responsible for the imbalance in the sex ratio found at contact probably played a role.

IV. The Population Problem at the Time of Contact

From the viewpoint of the population analyst, the shortage of women of reproductive ages could lead to serious problems of mating and group fertility. The view of the population analyst, however, is an etic or imposed conception and should not be confused with the emic definition of the situation as seen by the Mucajai Yanomama themselves. They did not view themselves as having a sex ratio problem as such. To perceive their situation in such a manner would have required thinking at the abstract level of the undifferentiated group, which they were unaccustomed to doing. It would also have required quantitative thought and calculation of a type to which they were unaccustomed.

What the population analyst might call "a sex ratio problem" was seen by the Yanomama in terms of family kinship and eligible marriage partners. Table 2.2 shows the age distribution and sex proportions for the two groups, the Borabuk and the Kaserapai. At this time marriages were only within the village. The Kaserapai had only four reproductive women. The men defined the "sex ratio" as a shortage of females with the correct kin relationship for marriage. It was not considered an extraordinary problem, as it arose from time to time in Yanomama villages. It is an example of the demographic volatility typical of small-sized villages. What was extraordinary about the Mucajai group at that time was their isolation from all other groups where women could be found. The problem was not seen as having any connection with preferential female infanticide. In later chapters we will discuss how balance between the sexes was restored.

The main preoccupation in the period just before contact was to obtain steel cutting tools such as knives and machetes. They were used in the preparation of fields, for making bows and arrows, and for hollowing out logs for canoes. Steel tools were not absolute necessities for subsistence; the Yanomama had traditional cutting tools made of stone and animal teeth. The steel tools were more efficient and enabled the Yanomama to develop better craftsmanship. They made life easier and more interesting. Previously such tools had been obtained by exchange with or raids upon other indigenous groups. But the Mucajai group had been isolated since the Maquiritare wars. The tools they had were wearing out and in need of replacement. They had moved to the banks of the Mucajai River in the hope of making contact with Brazilians from whom they could obtain the tools. At the time of contact this appeared to be their most preoccupying problem.

Three

Overview of the Postcontact Period, 1958–1987

The Mucajai population has grown, from 121 at the time of contact to 319 at the beginning of 1987, an increase of 198 people in 28 years. Figure 3.1 graphs the yearly population levels and the annual rates of increase. (The population size is the value at the beginning of the year and the rate represents the change from the beginning of that year to the beginning of the next.) Table 3.1 shows the same values for 5- and 10-year periods. Overall the postcontact period has an average annual growth rate of 3.5% (35 per 1000 population), a high rate of increase compared with other populations.

I. Rate of Growth and Its Components

Although there is an absolute increase in the population in all but 4 years, and although the average annual rate of increase for all 28 years is quite high, the yearly rates of increase are highly volatile. In the 6 years following contact, the average annual rate of increase was a slight 0.8%. Then it exploded to 5.0 and 5.2%, respectively, in the following 5-year periods, a rate higher than that of any modern

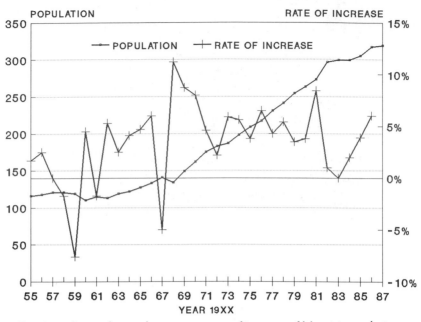

Fig. 3.1 Size and annual percentage rate of increase of Mucajai population.

Table 3.1
Size of Population and Average Annual Rate of Increase, 1958–1987

Year and date	Population	Average annual increase (%)		
		5 Years	10 Years	Total
1958 (11/9)	121			
		.78	2.64	
1965 (1/1)	127			
		4.98		
1970 (1/1)	162			
		5.22	4.96	3.5
1975 (1/1)	209			
		4.7		
1980 (1/1)	263			
		3.0	2.79	
1985 (1/1)	305			
		2.26		
1987 (1/1)	319			

nation. The rate began to decline around 1975 and continued the decline to 2.3% between 1985 and 1987. These variations in the rate of increase indicate the volatility of its demographic components.

A. Demographic Factors of Population Change

Table 3.2 shows the absolute and relative values of the four demographic components of population growth—births, deaths, in-migration, and out-migration. Group fertility is high, as expressed by the crude birth rate of 50 (per 1000 population, as are all crude rates.) Mortality reaches a moderately high level, as indicated by the crude death rate of 23. The interaction of these two gives a 2.7% annual rate of natural increase, a high rate compared with industrial populations. In-migration is significant, with a 10.4 crude rate. Out-migration is negligible, with a 1.3 crude rate. The interaction between the two gives a significant net migration of 9.1, especially when it is added to the rate of natural increase yielding the high 3.5% average annual rate of overall increase.

B. Age–Sex Structure of the Population

The variations in the annual rates of growth and their components change not only the size of the population, but also its age–sex structure. None of the four demographic components act in the same way for both sexes and for all ages of the life cycle. Births are restricted to the reproductive population. Certain ages are more prone to death than others. Since these are small-sized populations, a small absolute change in an age–sex segment of a population can cause a large change of the percentage that it comprises of the total population. This will become important because the altered age–sex structure feeds back on the demographic components themselves. Table 3.2 shows the change between the proportions of the age–sex segments of the population at contact and at the beginning of 1987.

II. Levels of Analysis and Demographic Indices

The upcoming chapters use demographic indices which can be considered at three different levels of analysis: the average individual in a defined group, a subgroup within the population, and the population

Table 3.2
Overview of Demographic Change

		Time periods			
	Precontact (pre-1958)	Contact (11/9/58)	Postcontact (1958–1986)	End of postcontact (1/1/87)	Change
Population		121		319	+198
r^a	−r		+3.5%		−/+
Crude birth			+50.1 (279)		
Crude death			−23.3 (132)		
Natural increase			+26.8 (147)		
Crude in-migration			+10.4 (58)		
Crude out-migration			−1.3 (7)		
Net migration			+9.1 (51)		
Age–sex					
Male		77		175	+ 98
Female		44		144	+100
% Male–Female		63.6%–36.4%		54.9%–45.1%	8.7%
r(male)			+3.0%		
r(female)			+4.3%		
% Male, age 0		15.7%		28.6%	+12.9%
% Female, age 0		14.9		20.4	+ 5.5
% Male, age 15		20.7		11.6	− 9.1
% Female, age 15		6.6		12.6	+ 6.0
% Male, age 30		19.0		6.9	+12.1
% Female, age 30		5.0		8.5	+ 3.5
% Male, age 45 +		8.3		8.2	− 0.1
% Female, age 45 +		9.9		3.1	− 6.8
Total		100.0%		100.0%	+ 3.5%

^{a}r, rate of increase.

itself. For analytical purposes it is important to distinguish these levels because they cannot be automatically projected from each other and, at times, may vary in opposite directions.

The fertility of the average reproductive female is expressed by the total fertility rate. The mortality level of the average individual within the population is expressed by the average life expectancy at birth. These are convenient summary measures taken from group schedules of either fertility or mortality and determined by them.

Fertility (maternity by convention) is restricted to a subgroup within the population, women between the ages of 15 and 44. Its level is expressed by the general fertility rate, which can be further specified by a schedule of 5-year age classes within this range.

At the level of the entire group, conventional demography employs rates called "crude" to measure the demographic variables. These are mathematical ratios of the incidence of the demographic events to the total number in the population regardless of its age–sex structure (therefore, "crude"). (In demographic convention, crude rates are not considered ratios, but in the mathematical sense they are.) These are simple rates to calculate. But beyond that, they are difficult to use by themselves in anthropological demography for comparing and understanding the source of any demographic change. The change in crude rates, as in any mathematical ratio, can come from a change in the numerator or the denominator or both, so long as they do not cancel each other out. The population value in the denominator of any crude rate has a specific age–sex structure. When two crude rates are compared to detect change or stability in the structure of fertility or mortality or migration, the proportions of the age–sex distributions of the two populations in the denominators must be the same. If these conditions are not met, then any difference between the crude rates can be due (1) exclusively to a change in structure of the demographic variable in the numerator, or (2) exclusively to differences of the age–sex proportions behind the population values used in the denominator, or (3) to a combination of the two. If only crude rates are available, as frequently is the case in anthropological demography, it is impossible to discriminate among these possibilities.

Because of these logical possibilities, conventional demography frequently makes a simplifying assumption. It assumes constancy of the age–sex proportions over time within a population or between populations. Therefore any change in the crude rate reflects only a change in the structure of the demographic variable in the numerator. This is a simplifying assumption because even though there may actually be differences in the age–sex proportions, it is assumed that in large populations these shifts are small and usually have only a slight influence on the ratio itself.

All disciplines are cultural artifacts, including conventional demography, which is strongly influenced by the structure of large-sized populations, mostly industrial societies (Early, 1982). Anthropological demography, when examining small-scale societies, usually cannot use the simplifying assumption that applies to large populations. Anthropological populations (as the term is used here) are small by definition. This means that demographic volatility is an essential characteristic. In the Mucajai population as shown in Table 3.2, the proportion of the reproductive population to the total population changed by 9.5% in the postcontact period. The classification of 0–14 years of age changed by 18.4%. Shifts of these magnitudes will have an impact on group fertility and mortality without necessarily changing the average level of individual fertility and mortality.

III. Terminology

The presentation of the research posed problems about the use of some technical words. Editorial decisions were made, some of which use terms with wider or narrower meanings than their literal or conventional usages. Some of these are noted here for clarification.

A. Sex Ratios

To express the balance or imbalance between the sexes in a population, the conventional expression is the sex ratio. This is the number of males divided by the number of females and multiplied by 100. This is actually a male ratio rather than a sex ratio as it easily tells the number of males for each female. When the females dominate, the meaning of its magnitude is not quickly intelligible. For this reason, this research will employ the proportion male or female, although it will sometimes be called a sex ratio. If the conventional sex ratio should be needed, it can be calculated from the proportion.

B. Population Values

The size of a population varies during a year. This research uses beginning-of-the-year and midyear values. The values for the beginning of the year are derived from the population registers. The month and day of migrations during the year are not known. Therefore midyear values were calculated by linear interpolation from beginning-of-the-year values.

C. Anthropological Demography and Anthropological Societies

These phrases are used in an older sense which is no longer accurate, but still adequate for the purposes here. Historically, cultural anthropology primarily studied small, nonliterate societies. Today cultural anthropology has spread its net to include many types of societies, a number of which are not small in size. No consensus has developed for a short, substitute phrase. Here, anthropological societies refer to those small-scale societies which have historically been studied by anthropologists. Anthropological demography is shorthand for the use of demographic methods by anthropologists for the study of these small-scale societies.

IV. Cultural Factors Responsible for the Demographic Variables and Age–Sex Structure

One of the purposes of this research is a demographic description of the structure and change of the Mucajai population. By itself this is an exercise of anthropological demography. But anthropological research should push further and connect the demographic variables with other aspects of the culture so as to attain an explanation of the population dynamics. In other words, the demography needs to be infused with ethnographic explanation. The demographic explanation is built around the "balancing equation" which states that any change in the size of a population is the result of a change in any one or combination of the four variables in the equation (fertility, mortality, in-migration, and out-migration). Cultural influences, in turn, work through one or several of these four demographic variables. Therefore the order of presentation will be (1) cultural (and sometimes biological) influences

responsible for the magnitude and structure of each demographic variable. Fertility is examined in Chapter 4, in-migration and out-migration in Chapter 6, and mortality in Chapter 7. Chapter 5 is a methodological chapter dealing with the problem of age estimation. (2) The
interaction of the four demographic variables to determine the size
and age–sex structure of a population and its change, which are discussed in Chapter 8. But since the size and age–sex structure of a
population affect, in turn, the intensity of some cultural patterns,
Chapter 9 asks (3) how the changes in the size of the population and/
or the demographic variables affect cultural patterns.

V. Phases of the Postcontact Period

This research is primarily concerned with the postcontact period of
the Mucajai group from November 9, 1958 to January 1, 1987. This
was a period of demographic flux. The problem is how to subdivide
this period so that the classifications are not arbitrary groupings, but
capable of distinguishing the heterogeneity of the population dynamics. An inspection was made of the graphs of the annual crude birth,
in-migration, and death rates for the period (Figs. 4.2, 6.1, 7.1). All
suggest the same divisions: the immediate postcontact period from
1958 to 1969, the intermediate period from 1970 to 1979, and the
final phase from 1980 to 1986.

VI. The Missionaries

During the discussion of the postcontact period, mention will be made
of the missionaries. For the purposes of this study their role needs to
be made explicit. How much change did the missionaries introduce
into traditional Yanomama culture? What influence did they have on
the demographic structure? Since these questions can be better answered after presenting some ethnographic and demographic data,
they will be taken up in Chapter 8.

Another question concerns the missionaries as a source of demographic information. A brief description of the mission follows so that
its role as such a source can be better evaluated. The purpose of the
mission was to establish a church based on an evangelical interpreta-

tion of the Bible. Four American or Canadian missionaries lived at the station for this purpose. Historically these have been two married couples, or a married couple and two single persons. At any one time only two or three were actually in residence due to absences for personal or business reasons. One of the men served as the administrator and as a Bible teacher for the Mucajai men. Another person was a linguist responsible for translating the Bible into Ninam. The other two served as Bible teachers, men with men and women with women. Literacy classes were also conducted for this purpose. Beyond these strictly religious functions, the mission also had a dispensary for medical needs and a trading store where the Mucajai sold or traded local items and received manufactured goods. A small dirt airstrip provided communication with the regional capital in Boa Vista.

Two residences were built for the missionaries. The sides and floors were made of palm slats. Palm leaves were originally used for the roofs, although in later years these were replaced by sheets of aluminum. The houses were built on stilts to provide better ventilation. The door of each residence opened into a gathering room for the Yanomama. The living quarters of the missionaries occupied the remainder of the house. Medicine was kept in one of the residences with the gathering room also serving as a dispensary. Later a separate building was constructed for dispensing medicine and treating the sick. Those with serious medical problems were flown out to Boa Vista and sometimes to the larger Brazilian medical centers. A shed was constructed to house tools for maintenance of the residences and the airstrip. It also became the store for trade goods. For formal gatherings, such as the weekly church meeting, the space created by the pilings beneath the residences was used.

The mission became an important center of Yanomama life. It was the one place where people from all the village-houses would congregate. Every day Yanomama would come to the gathering rooms for medical reasons, to help with biblical translation, to exchange goods at the trading post, or simply to socialize. The tool shed became a male "hangout." Compared with industrial society, the pace of life was slow. Many would linger and chat for long periods of time. Village happenings were thoroughly narrated and discussed. The Yanomama have a characteristic common to many small-scale societies: every villager's personal life is a matter of public scrutiny and discussion. It was in this context that the missionaries, all of whom spoke Ninam,

learned about births, deaths, migrations, and infanticides. In numer-
ous cases of death and for some births, the missionaries would be summoned to the village-houses to render medical assistance. This social
interaction allowed easy conversation about births and deaths. The
missionaries also spent considerable time in the village-houses where
the same information was also learned or could be verified. It was a
small, relatively close-knit community with the missionaries becom-
ing an integral part of it. This happened in spite of the fact that after
an initial period of interest, the majority of the Yanomama either
explicitly rejected the religious activity of the missionaries or were
indifferent to it. They still came to the mission station for socializing,
medical attention, occasional employment in maintenance, and to
obtain trade goods. In these activities the missionaries made no distinction between believers and nonbelievers.

This was the communal setting in which the demographic information was obtained. The Yanomama knew the missionaries had an interest in them and were recording births and deaths. There is no strict
cultural prohibition about mentioning the dead as in other Yanomama
regions. A close relative might have some hesitation talking about a
death and only use the kin term for someone recently deceased, never
the name of the person. In the single-house villages, many others
would also know of deaths including those of infants. In the chapters
to come, the verb "report" will sometimes be used as a summary label
for the gathering of information. This should be understood in its
proper context and does not imply a formal reporting system.

PART TWO

Cultural and Demographic Structures of the Population Variables

Four

The Reproductive Period

There have been 279 births in the Mucajai community in the postcontact period, 144 male and 135 female. To understand Yanomama reproduction, this chapter examines the mating pattern, the female reproductive pattern, and the demographic levels of fertility.

I. Mating Pattern

All postpubertal women in the database except one have entered a formal sexual union at least once. Widows still in their fertile years quickly enter another formal union, although there are several exceptions which have been taken into account in the analysis.

A. Mate Selection

Mate selection is partially determined by the kinship system of the Yanomama, which approximates a general type known in the anthropological literature as a cross-cousin or a bifucate merging system (Chagnon, 1983; Lizot, 1988). An explanation of this system would be lengthy and distract from the main purpose of this presentation.

Mention will be made here of only those aspects that help explain mate selection.

The Yanomama kinship system is classificatory as it links every member of the village to each other by a kin relationship. The system distinguishes cross and parallel cousins. The parallel cousins are the children of father's brothers (father–brother is same or parallel sex) and the children of mother's sisters (same or parallel sex). They belong to the same lineage and the kin term used between them is "brother" or "sister," the same as that used for biological siblings. Marriage is forbidden between parallel cousins. It is considered incestuous because it is within the same lineage. Cross cousins are the children of father's sisters (father–sister is cross sex) and the children of mother's brothers (cross sex). They belong to different lineages and ego must choose a mate who is related as a cross cousin (called "wanima" in Ninam). The cross or parallel sex consideration is not restricted to the parental generation, but considers prior and subsequent generations. Through the convergence or divergence of descent lines, everyone in ego's generation in the village is either a parallel or a cross cousin.

The preferred female for union is a bilateral cross cousin, i.e., one who is at one and the same time the daughter of father's sister and the daughter of mother's brother. Within the Yanomama social system, the primary sexual union determines many other social relationships which, in complex societies, are distinct institutional processes, economic, political, military, etc. The bilateral cross-cousin union is preferred because such a marital union affirms the social bonds between two wife-giving kin groups.

The second pattern of mate preference is sister exchange arranged by two single men who are not closely related. This also creates or strengthens the bonds between two family groups who become wife givers on equal terms.

It is not always possible to arrange the preferred types of union. The male then must seek a female who is cross-cousin to him in other ways. In all these instances of cross-cousin marriages, the male provides the gifts and service to the bride's family. Women captured in raids on enemy groups and brought back to the village as prisoners also become wives. There are no kinship requirements or obligations of gifts and service to the bride's family when this occurs.

B. Petition and Betrothal

Once a youth has become a capable hunter he may petition a girl's parents and her brothers. Parents may also betroth their children while they are still infants. The petitions are usually made during the community feasts while the men are using hallucinogenic drugs. The discussion includes promises of gifts and work service from the husband-to-be. Sometimes the petition occurs informally apart from festive occasions. A few weeks later the husband-to-be will leave fresh game at the hearth of the girl's family. The preparing, cooking, and eating of the game by the girl's mother signals the acceptance of the petition. Once betrothed, the girl is seen as the property of her husband. Any infringement of this status by the girl leads to serious conflict with the boy's family. If the boy should die before cohabitation, the girl is considered a widow. Although the word "betrothed" has been used, it implies some of the obligations of marriage itself in other cultures.

C. Bride Service and Gifts

With betrothal the male owes gifts and service to the family of the girl. In the postcontact period the presents consisted of trade goods such as axes, knives, beads, clothing, aluminum pots, and hammocks. These replaced cotton, arrow tips, arrows, and loincloths of the precontact period. Meat (bird, fish, monkey, leg of peccary or tapir) must be given at least once a month. Provision of game is the most important duty of betrothal and it symbolizes the future husband's fulfillment of his service to the girl's family. When he returns from the hunt and distributes the meat, his first obligation is to the girl's family. Beginning with cohabitation, the young man usually spends a period of up to several years living with the girl's family and performing bride service. He continues to hunt for her family, helps them build canoes, and aids them in preparing the garden. If the girl's family engages in conflict within the village or is involved in a raid on another village, the future husband must provide physical assistance. At the end of this period the young man may choose to remain, although more often he will move his family to the area or village of his own kin group.

A betrothal may be broken if the male ceases providing his services or if he becomes publicly involved with another woman. If the girl becomes involved with another male, she will be scolded and beaten by her parents and brothers in an effort to maintain the betrothal and its incoming gifts. If this fails, there may be violence between the two families to resolve disputes over return of bridal gifts. Even if there is no question of misconduct, conflicts may arise over the regularity of gifts.

D. Sexual Unions and Recognition of Paternity

The core of Yanomama social structure consists of a sexual union between a cohabiting couple (husband–wife). The wife may have other recognized sexual unions with the consent of the husband. The most frequent case of wife sharing is with the husband's younger brother. A younger brother, until he acquires his own wife, has a quasi-right to the wife of an older brother although at times it may be contested. The husband may also consent to share his wife with other males. These wife-sharing arrangements are usually formally recognized relationships and relatively stable. Some men remain secondary husbands their entire lives. Others become a primary husband following the death of the former primary husband.

Wife-sharing has specific implications for socially recognized paternity with its obligations of support, especially for supplying meat. In Mucajai ethnophysiology, embryos result exclusively from male semen and require multiple acts of insemination. The embryo not only is made by the male semen, but requires semen for its nourishment. Where more than one man is having sexual relations with a woman, the semen of each male is perceived as helping to make and nourish the embryo. A similar ethnophysiology has been found among other Amazonian populations: the Mundurucu (Murphy and Murphy, 1974), the Tapirape (Wagley, 1977), the Kraho (Melatti, 1979), the Mehinaku, and the Kuikuru (Gregor, 1985).

All males who have contributed to the making and growth of the embryo are designated as fathers of the child. The primary husband of the woman is also the principal father unless a birth occurs when it is known that he could not have been the father. He bears the primary obligations of paternity, but may request assistance from the other fathers. If the primary father dies or is unable to fulfill his obligations, the other fathers take responsibility for their children. A secondary father who has supplied meat for his female child also has the right to be consulted about her betrothal petitions. The biological genitor of a child with several recognized fathers is unknown and socially irrelevant.

There are also sexual unions that involve recognized paternity but no marriage. Separated or widowed women give birth without having a primary husband. Clandestine affairs outside marriage result in pregnancy and birth. These affairs seldom remain completely clandestine, with the fathers usually known and recognized. There was only one case of a mother who never entered into a primary husband–wife relationship.

II. Female Reproductive Period

There is a pattern of reproduction among Yanomama women that is striking in its regularity for almost all the women in the group. This section gives an ethnographic account of the pattern followed by a quantitative description.

A. First Menstruation and Menopause

These biological markers indicate the potential beginning and end of reproduction. The first menstruation takes place between 12 and 13 years of age (average of 12.4 years with standard error of .18 for 21 recorded cases). To signify the occasion, the girl's family erects a small leaf enclosure within the communal dwelling (yano). Her hair is cut close to the scalp with bamboo arrow tips (or scissors). She remains isolated in the enclosure and only her mother and sisters will whisper to her. No male may see or converse with her, or even mention her name. The female members of the family feed her and accompany her outside for baths and other necessities. When her hair has returned to normal length, she abandons the enclosure and resumes her normal activities. This rite of passage marks the transition from childhood to womanhood.

The average age at menopause appears to be in the first half of the 40s. This estimate is based on the average age of 39.9 years at last birth of women who have completed childbearing.

B. Cohabitation

The girl may live with her family for up to 2 years after the puberty rite. The families decide when cohabitation should begin. Her family invites the young man to whom she has been betrothed and his family for an extended hunting-gathering trip in the jungle. One day the girl's mother remains behind while the rest of the group is foraging. She removes the hammock of the young man from its place with his family and ties it above the girl's hammock among those of her own family. When the young man returns, he feigns surprise and reclines in his relocated hammock. The girl reclines in hers and this symbolizes the onset of cohabitation. As the girl is still young and often afraid, coitus may not occur for 2–6 weeks, until she has been instructed and encouraged by her mother. The young man takes up residence with the girl's family and provides game for them.

C. Pregnancy

Cohabitation occurs around the age of 13 or 14 years for the female. The Yanomama consider this to be too young to become a mother because the reproductive organs are still developing. A 9-month gestation and birth could damage them and thereby endanger future pregnancies and births. Yet no effective measures are taken to prevent conception. If a young girl should become pregnant too soon after beginning cohabitation, an abortion is induced with the assistance of her mother or possibly her mother-in-law. In the postcontact period, 5.4% of first births were known to be preceded by an induced abortion for this reason.

D. First Birth

The average age at first birth is 16.8 years. In cases of previous abortion, the average is 17.1 years. When a girl is ready for delivery, her mother, mother-in-law, and her sisters and any young children in their care accompany her a short distance into the jungle. There she sits on a fallen log with women seated on each side of her and holding her legs. Banana leaves are placed on the ground between the mother's legs. When the delivery begins, another woman stands behind the mother and pushes carefully on the upper abdomen. As the birth occurs, the infant slides onto the banana leaves without being touched. A bamboo stick is used to cut the umbilical cord and the placenta is buried. The dull edge of the stick has a cauterizing effect and the bleeding soon stops. The baby is taken up by one of the helpers, who washes it with water an then gives it to the mother before the group returns to the village.

E. The Problem of the Nursling and Its Effect on the Spacing of
Additional Births

The day after the birth the mother resumes her work routine of gathering manioc in the garden and firewood in the jungle. During these trips away from the village the infant is taken along and nursed or occasionally left in the care of the grandmother or an older sister.

In the Yanomama view, the newborn infant will live only if it is able to suckle its mother's breast until the eruption of the infant's back molars. This gives the infant the capacity to chew sufficient food for its own nourishment. Until this time, the infant is dependent on the mother's milk. The back teeth erupt at approximately 2 to 2.25 years of age. Before this time, the mother may masticate small amounts of bananas or papaya and together with juice of sweet potato or meat broth, supplement her milk. If there is no reason to stop the breastfeeding, it may continue into the fourth or even the fifth year.

Early weaning is seen as a probable cause of an infant's death. The Yanomama perceive the mother's milk supply as an unchanging amount, all of which is required by the nursling. Any threat to the mother's milk is defined as a threat to the life of the nursling itself. One such threat would be another birth before 2 to 2.25 years of the previous surviving birth. The available means to avoid such a birth are postpartum restraint and induced abortion. There is a cultural norm that a mother should refrain from sexual relations until the nursling's back teeth have erupted. However, this restriction is not carefully followed and sexual relations are frequently resumed after 6 months or a year. As there is no contraception, any new pregnancies leading to a birth within this period are aborted. As will be seen in Chapter 7, this is the most important cause of abortion among the Mucajai Yanomama.

The biological view of reproduction confirms some of the Yanomama ethnophysiology. Breastfeeding has a contraceptive effect due to the release of hormones by the suckling action of the infant (Konner and Worthman, 1980; Anderson, 1983; Short, 1984). The effect of the hormone is continual for a Yanomama mother because the infant is suckled on demand and sleeps with the mother so that the breast is constantly available. By Bongaart's equation (Bongaarts and Potter, 1983), the contraceptive effect should last an average of 18 months when breastfeeding endures for 2.25 years. Since the duration of the contraceptive effect is shorter than the duration of breastfeeding itself, the lactating mother may become pregnant. When there is a pregnancy which would result in a birth after the nursling is old enough to be independent of the mother's milk, the pregnancy will usually be allowed to go to term. The Yanomama are not fully aware of the contraceptive effect of breastfeeding. Since postpartum restraint is more likely to be observed during the first part of the lactation period, the effect is partially concealed. Moreover, individual women show wide variations from the average duration of the contraceptive effect, which obscures easy discernment.

The duration of spacings between successive registered births can be derived from the fertility histories which were reconstructed for each mother in the database. There are 188 such intervals. In 133

Table 4.1
Length of Regular Birth Intervals

Years between births	Number of intervals	%	C %[a]
1.0	1	0.8	0.8
1.2	0	0.0	0.8
1.4	0	0.0	0.8
1.6	2	1.5	2.3
1.8	2	1.5	3.8
2.0	10	7.5	11.3
2.2	7	5.3	16.6
2.4	11	8.3	24.9
2.6	14	10.5	35.4
2.8	11	8.3	43.7
3.0	12	9.0	52.7
3.2	16	12.0	64.7
3.4	14	10.5	75.2
3.6	9	6.8	82.0
3.8	4	3.0	85.0
4.0	5	3.8	88.8
4.2	2	1.5	90.3
4.4	4	3.0	93.3
4.6	0	0.0	93.3
4.8	2	1.5	94.8
5.0	3	2.3	97.1
5.2	0	0.0	97.1
5.4	2	1.5	98.6
5.6	0	0.0	98.6
5.8	2	1.5	100.0
Total	133	100.0	

[a]C%, cumulative percent.

of these intervals, between the previous child and the birth under consideration, there was no intervening pregnancy ending in either abortion or infant death before 2.25 years. These will be called regular intervals. Table 4.1 and Fig. 4.1 show the spacing between these births. Seventy percent of the intervals are between 2 and 3.5 years as expected from the ethnographic data on fertility. There is a single interval of 1 year in which the infant was immediately killed because of the short spacing from the nursling. There is less than 2 years of spacing in 3% of the cases, in which the nursling was apparently weaned early. Classifying the intervals by sibling order in Table 4.2 shows little discrimination. Each of the first four orders has an average duration of approximately 3.1 years. Beginning with the interval between the fifth and sixth child, it lengthens to 3.4 years, which it approximates for the rest of the reproductive period. Maintaining an average birth interval of about 3 years to protect the nursling may have the effect of guaranteeing the relatively quick onset of the next pregnancy with age of the mother playing a relatively minor role. It appears to be distinctive of this type of reproductive pattern.

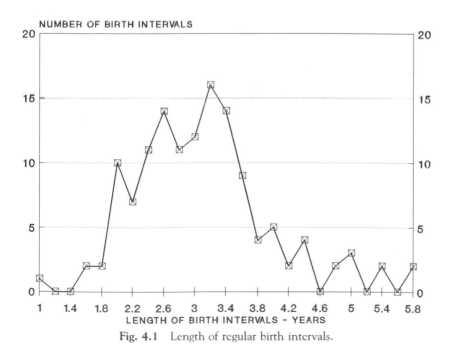

Fig. 4.1 Length of regular birth intervals.

Table 4.2
Average Duration of Regular Birth Intervals by Sibling Order;
Standard Error and Standard Deviation

Sibling order	Duration (years)			n
	Average	S.E.	S.D.	
1–2	3.1	.16	.8	27
2–3	3.0	.17	.8	23
3–4	3.1	.19	.9	22
4–5	3.1	.23	.9	15
5–6	3.4	.24	1.0	18
6–7	3.4	.29	1.0	13
7–8	3.0	.38	1.0	7
8–9	3.6	.58	1.3	5
9–10	3.1	1.34	1.9	2
Total				133

III. Types of Birth Intervals and Their Duration

There are other types of birth intervals in addition to the regular interval just described. This section classifies these intervals, employing as criteria the reasons for their varying durations. Most are factors of fetal or demographic mortality (a mortality preceded by a birth) as shown in Table 4.3. The typology yields further insight into the structure of reproduction. It is also used in the next chapter as the basis for determining the age of those whose birth dates were not registered.

Table 4.3
Types and Average Duration of Registered Birth Intervals; Standard Error and Standard Deviation

Type of interval	Duration (years)			n	%
	Average	S.E.	S.D.		
Death, <1 mo.	1.9	.21	.8	16	8.5
Death, 1–27 mo.	2.1	.17	.6	14	7.4
Regular	3.2	.08	.9	133	70.7
With abortion	3.8	.36	1.3	14	7.4
With stillbirth	4.1	.36	.8	6	3.2
Extended	8.3	2.45	4.8	5	2.7
Total				188	100

The shortest type of interval with an average duration of 1.9 years contains the death of an infant of age 1 month or less (neonatal death). Most of these died in the first hours of life and include infanticides (infanticides and abortion will be treated in more detail in Chapter 7). This obviates the need for nursing the infant so that conception may occur sooner than in a regular interval. This pregnancy is usually allowed to go to term since it is not competing with the nursling.

The second type contains an infant or child death between 1 month and 2.25 years. The structure of this interval is the same as the previous except that the mean duration, 2.1 years, is longer because the intervening dead infant survived for a longer period.

The third type is the regular interval in which the preceding nursling survives until it is capable of masticating its food, i.e., until it is no longer dependent on the mother's breast.

The fourth type of interval contains an intentional abortion. These are performed around the end of the second or beginning of the third month of pregnancy. Protection of a nursling is the principal reason for abortion, but additional reasons will be discussed in Chapter 7. An abortion increases the length of the interval because of the time for carrying the embryo plus the time for pregnancy to reoccur. Such an interval is about 6 months longer than the regular interval.

The fifth type of interval contains a stillbirth or miscarriage which usually occurs in the last 3 months of the pregnancy. The duration of the pregnancy of the miscarried fetus adds an average of 3.5 months to the interval.

The last type of interval has been labeled "extended." These are several long intervals for which the unusual reason is known. Some are in-migrating widows from non-Mucajai villages who came into the group to remarry with a hiatus in sexual activity during the transition. Others are unusual cases of widows who did not enter another formal union.

IV. Reproductive Pattern: Age and Overall Levels of Fertility

The frequency of births at various ages relative to the size of the female population of these ages is expressed by age-specific fertility rates presented in Table 4.4. In the averages for the entire postcontact period

Table 4.4
Fertility Rates: Total Fertility (Average Number of Live Births), Age-Specific, General, and
Crude Births per 1000 Population

Level of analysis	Type of rate	Age	Phase 1	Phase 2	Phase 3	2 + 3	Total
Average individual	Total fertility	—	8.7	7.5	7.5	7.5	7.9
Reproductive population	Age-specific (per 1000 population)	15	272	260	266	262	266
		20	240	322	259	294	272
		25	363	306	246	278	289
		30	258	276	283	279	277
		35	300	197	252	230	243
		40	313	140	190	169	217
	General fertility	15–44	279	275	256	265	268
Group	Crude birth	—	40.0	54.1	50.6		49.9
Births (n)	Male		26	59	59		144 (52%)
	Female		34	55	46		135 (48%)
	Total		60	114	105		279

(last column), the rates to age 35 show little variation. In graphic
terms, it is a relatively flat curve, while the profile of such rates for
other groups usually has a much more pronounced rise from age 15
to an age of peak fertility, somewhere in the twenties, and a more
pronounced decline from this peak over the remaining reproductive
years. The small variation is primarily due to the first phase, which
had an unusual age structure. It was strongly influenced by the mortality and in-migration of that period. As a result of infectious disease
brought back from Brazilian peasants by the early downstream trips,
many of the women over 20 years of age were dying. Shortly thereafter
there was a large influx of captive and other in-migrant women who
began bearing children according to the accustomed pattern. In others
words, during this period there was a small number of women and
most of them were either dying or giving birth. The eight births of
this phase were by five mothers. For this reason, Table 4.4 also gives
an average for the last two phases only. These figures give a closer
approximation of the expected shape of a curve of age-specific fertility.
The peak rate appears between the ages of 20 and 24. It remains high
to age 34 and then shows a precipitous decline in the late thirties and
early forties.

CRUDE BIRTH RATE PER 1000 POPULATION

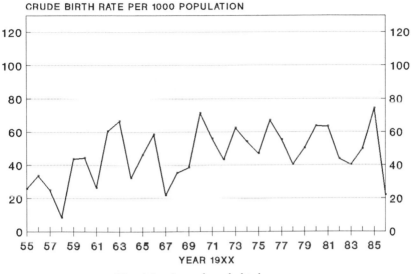

Fig. 4.2 Annual crude birth rates.

The total fertility rate indicates the average number of live births to a woman who lives through her entire reproductive period. In the first phase it was 8.7 children, while 7.5 was the average for the last two phases. For reasons already mentioned, the higher rate for the first phase will be seen as one of a range within the same reproductive pattern and not as a change of the pattern itself. Consequently, the reproductive pattern will be considered relatively constant over the three phases. The general fertility rate shows this constancy. This is a rate for the female reproductive population, regardless of the age distribution of the women within it.

The crude birth rate is the rate for the whole population. Figure 4.2 graphs the rate for each year and shows its volatility with a post-contact range of 8 to 75 per 1000 population. In addition to small numbers, another reason for the volatility is the reproductive pattern itself. After a year of high fertility, there are proportionately fewer women available to give birth because of the postpartum protection of the nursling. After this period they become pregnant again. There-fore there is frequently a steep up–down pattern.

V. Summary

This chapter has examined the reproductive pattern of Ninam Yanomama women. The age at betrothal-marriage is young, sometimes before puberty. Menstruation takes place at an average age of 12.4 years.
Cohabitation begins sometime within the next 2 years. First birth occurs at an average of 16.8 years. A pregnancy leading to a birth earlier
than this is often terminated by induced abortion. The average
woman has between seven and eight live births during her reproductive period. Fertility is not higher because of lengthy lactation and
sometimes induced abortion, which extend birth intervals to a duration of 2 to 3.5 years. These practices are primarily used to protect
the life of the nursling. They are not perceived as fertility control
measures in the sense that fewer children are considered necessary or
desirable.

Table 4.5 shows the average age of the mother at each phase of the
reproductive cycle. The age at menarche is derived from 21 cases
where both date of birth and date of the puberty ceremony were recorded by the missionaries. The ages of mothers at the first three birth
orders are calculated from cases where the birth dates of both mother
and infant were registered. There were few or no registered cases for
the higher orders. The average age at the fourth birth was derived by
adding the average duration of the regular interval for the fourth birth

Table 4.5
Average Age of Women at Phases of Reproductive
Period

Reproductive structure	Average age (years)	Source
Menarche	12.4	21 cases
1 birth	16.8	21 cases
2 births	19.9	13 cases
3 births	22.4	6 cases
4 births	26.0	Estimated
5 births	29.1	Estimated
6 births	32.5	Estimated
7 births	35.9	Estimated
8 births	38.8	Estimated
9 births	42.4	Estimated

to the average age at the third birth. This process was repeated for each higher sibling order.

The first two births are usually to mothers in their teens or just entering the twenties, followed by three during the twenties and three during the thirties to mothers of average parity. Women of higher-than-average parity may continue the reproductive period into their forties. Higher parities can also result from infanticide and infant mortality because the intervals are shortened as indicated in Table 4.3. Using 12 fertility histories where the mother had passed menopause, 39.9 years was the average age of the mother at the time of her last child and 8 was the average number of live births during the reproductive period. This gives information about an actual cohort of women born before contact, while the age-specific rates reflect synthetic cohorts. Their close agreement confirms the constancy of the fertility structure.

This quantitative analysis of the reproductive period shows that a Yanomama woman spends most of her time between 16 and 42 years of age either pregnant or nursing. The average reproductive period including the nursing of the last sibling is 26 years. (Average age at first birth is 16.8 years, less the 9 months of pregnancy means starting around 16. The average age at the average last birth is 39.9 years plus 2.25 years for lactation gives about 42 years.) An average of eight live births means 72 months or 6 years of pregnancy and 18 years of lactation. Therefore the average mother is pregnant or nursing for 24 of the 26 years, or 92% of her reproductive years. Primary sterility is rare. The database contains only one woman past 30 who has had no births and apparently no pregnancies of any duration.

Five

Determination of Age

This chapter explains how a birth date for the calculation of age was determined for each individual in the population. Age data have appeared in the preceding chapters, but explanation of the methodology has been postponed to this chapter because it is based on the Yanomama reproductive pattern described in the previous chapter.

I. The Anthropological Problem of Age

Determining the age of people in anthropological or nonliterate populations poses a difficult and frequently impossible problem. It is one of the principal reasons for the relatively few demographic analyses of population dynamics in anthropological literature. Age as a measure of a life span assumes a unit of measurement and a counting system, both of which are cultural conventions. Western societies employ the cyclical relationship between the earth and the sun to measure time and they also use a unitary counting system which can handle the smallest to the largest numbers. By contrast, the Yanomama employ the cyclical relationship between the moon and the earth for their infrequent measurements of time. Their counting system identifies only three measured units—one, two, and a residual category "many," which simply means more than two. Individuals do not know their age because there is no need for it, and there are no written records. The difficulties of estimating age exclusively from physical appearances are well known, especially in a culture alien to the investigator.

An ideal solution would be an observer living in the group for a lengthy period of time and functioning as a demographic scribe, noting births, deaths, and migrations. In the case of the Mucajai Yanomama, this role has been played by the missionaries since the first permanent contact in late 1958. The database contains records of the 463 people who have lived in the Mucajai population since then. As indicated in the first column of Table 5.1, the dates of birth for 273 of these (59%) were registered by the missionaries. Consequently there are no problems regarding age for over half the database used for this research. The estimation problem concerns the other 190 people (41%) who lived at sometime in the postcontact population. These

Table 5.1
Sources of Birth Dates of Postcontact Population

		Source of birth date				
			Estimated			
Year of birth	Registered	R-SE[a]	R-Chain[b]	E[c]	E-Chain[d]	Total
Before 1900			1	1	5	7
1900–1909			7		3	10
1910–1919			7	1	6	14
1920–1929			11	4	9	24
1930–1939			13	9	5	27
1940–1949		3	34	4		41
1950–1959	3	16	20	2	1	42
1960–1969	52	10	5	2		69
1970–1979	117	1	2			120
1980–1986	101	5	3			109
Total	273	35	103	23	29	463
%	59.0	7.6	22.2	5.0	6.3	100

[a]Estimating average subtracted from a registered birth date.
[b]Estimating average subtracted from a previously estimated birth date by iteration.
[c]Ethnohistorical estimation.
[d]Estimating average subtracted from a previously estimated (from ethnohistorical data) birth date by iteration.

include 121 born before contact, 58 who in-migrated, and 11 whose exact dates of birth were not recorded either because they lived downstream or were late-recorded infanticides. An estimation of the date of birth for these individuals is needed in order to compute age-specific demographic measures.

II. Estimation of Birth Dates from Fertility Histories

Both the ethnographic and the quantitative data of the previous chapter have established the patterned regularity of the female reproductive period. The biological clock underlying human reproduction ticks with a highly predictable rhythm, especially in this small, homogeneous population where there is minimal cultural interference to upset the timing. The major constraint is the postpartum protection of the nursling, which also follows its own rhythm. These regularities are shown by the small standard errors of the spacing averages in Tables 4.4 and 4.5. The result is patterned, highly predictable behavior which is the foundation of the age estimates.

Fertility histories were compiled for all mothers in the database. The offspring were listed in order of birth which had been established from the registered birth date, census, or genealogy. The sibling order in a family can also be determined by the kinship terms of address used between siblings. This helps clarify ambiguities.

All registered births in the fertility histories were then assigned their dates of birth. Wherever successive registered birth dates occur in a history, the duration of the spacing between them was calculated. These birth intervals were then classified by types and the averages and standard errors were computed for each type (Table 4.4). The intervals lacking dates were classified in the same way and their duration projected from the mean of the same type derived from registered intervals. This estimated duration is then subtracted from the birth date of the next older sibling to give an estimated birth date.

There were 104 fertility histories (including 4 nonmigrants who were mothers of in-migrants). Forty-nine histories had a registered birth date for all children. Most of these mothers have not yet reached menopause. Twenty-five of the histories had at least one registered date among the children, usually the later birth orders since these occurred after contact. Beginning with the earliest registered child in a history, the type of spacing between it and the previous child was noted. The average duration for this type was then subtracted from the registered birth date to estimate the birth date of the previous child. If there were additional unregistered siblings in the same history, the same procedure was iterated back to the first child. Table 5.1 distinguishes two kinds of estimates. If the estimating average was subtracted from a registered birth date, this is noted as method R-SE because confidence limits could be measured by the standard deviation. If the estimating average was subtracted from a previously estimated birth date by iteration, this has been designated as R-Chain in Table 5.1. The R means that a chain of estimated values was used beginning from a registered date.

There were 19 fertility histories of women born before 1940 without any registered birth dates, but which had at least one female in them who later became a mother and consequently had her own fertility history. The date of birth of her first child, either registered or estimated, was found and from this was subtracted 16.8 years, the average age at first birth for the 21 cases where both age of mother and first child were registered. This gave the date of birth of at least one female. These are R-SE or R-Chain depending on registration or estimation of the first child. The remaining siblings in the history were then estimated in the same way as in histories with at least one registered date. If a history contains two or more females who later became mothers, each series was calculated and the one with the best fit with surrounding histories or an average between the two series was employed.

There were 11 fertility histories of women born before 1915 which contained neither registered birth dates nor a female who later became a Mucajai mother. The date of birth of one person in each history was estimated by ethnohistorical data employing a memory calendar composed of events and dates in the other histories that could be related to the person. These are designated E (ethnohistorical) in Table 5.1. The birth dates of the remaining siblings were estimated from this one by the chain logic already described and designated E-Chain in Table 5.1. There were a few elderly males and male in-migrants not listed in any of the fertility histories. They were also estimated by the ethnohistorical data and designated E in the table.

Fifteen of the histories of women born before 1920 were considered incomplete because they contained less than five children and it was known that the mother did not die during her reproductive period. Therefore spacing averages could not be used for the other siblings from the first one estimated. In these cases the years comprising the mother's reproductive span were estimated. The number of years in the reproductive span was divided by the number of siblings in the history and the siblings were distributed by this factor over the years of the reproductive span (linear interpolation). Most of these individuals died before contact and for purposes here, the results concern a few of the oldest people in the population at the time of contact. These are E-Chain.

An assumption of all these methods is that there has been no change in the fertility structure from the precontact to the postcontact period. Ethnographic investigation has confirmed that the customs connected with childbearing have remained the same in the two periods.

III. Evaluation of the Averages as Estimators

In the calculation of the demographic age rates, almost 60% of the postcontact population have a registered date. Therefore the estimation process concerned only 40% of the population, most of whom were born before contact. In the preceding description of the information available in the various types of fertility histories, the histories that go further back in time are subject to greater possibilities of error. The analytical variable that will be most affected is the age at death. Age-specific fertility rates do not encompass the whole life cycle and consequently do not go as far back in time as mortality rates.

The validity of using the averages in Tables 4.3 and 4.4 as the basis of estimating birth dates depends on two principal considerations. The first is the purposes for which the estimations are to be used and therefore how much estimation error can be tolerated. The other consideration looks at the statistical characteristics of the distributions generating the average to find out the probable range of the estimation error.

The ages from the estimated dates of birth will be used in age rates of fertility, mortality, and migration. The age schedules of these rates collapse the data in two ways so that exact age is never required. The age schedules employ 10-year age groupings, except fertility which

uses 5-year groupings. In addition, the postcontact years have been
grouped into phases of 11-, 10-, and 7-year periods. This two-way
grouped classification is robust and can tolerate estimation error in the
ages entering into the calculations. At any point in the research where
exact data with no estimation error are required, only registered data
are used.

The standard error of the estimate gives an indication of the range
of possible error of measurement as a result of using the spacing means.
The smaller the standard error, the more precise is the use of the
mean for estimation. Tables 4.3 and 4.4 show the standard errors. The
averages used for estimation range from .15 to .4 of a year (1 month,
24 days to 4 months, 24 days). This means that when employing the
average as a single estimator for the unregistered birth dates, the actual value of the mean in about two-thirds of the R-SE cases will fall
one standard error above or below the mean.

The more difficult problem is the one-third of the population whose
birth dates were obtained by a chain of estimations. Here error may
become cumulative. The worst possible case is the highly unlikely
accumulation of all the estimation errors in the same direction. The
best possible case is random cancellation by which error in one direction is exactly offset by error in the opposite direction. Statistically,
most estimations would lie somewhere between these extremes.

The possibility of some estimation error was a constant concern
when linkages were used to estimate the birth dates of the older people
in the database. No estimated birth date was accepted solely at face
value. In a number of cases, an individual's birth date could be estimated in several ways from genealogical and biological relationships.
Most were estimated by the methods previously described where the
fewest estimators between the registered date and the estimated date
were required.

Additional cross-checking was done. Within a genealogical matrix,
the estimated value is surrounded by related values, all of which
should be consistent with each other. The estimated dates were always
compared with surrounding data. Dates for the same person derived
by alternative linkages were also checked to see if they were consistent
and reasonable. Adjustments of several years were made in some cases
to make a series of dates more consistent. In one instance, some large
inconsistencies were encountered between several related groups. Detailed examination indicated a possible error in recording the kin relationship between two women in the genealogies. The estimated birth

dates indicated what the correct relationship should be. An inquiry was sent to Brazil and the Yanomama verified that the correct rela-tionship between the two women was that predicted from the esti-mated birth dates. These different ways of checking the data allowed control of cumulative error.

IV. Completeness of the Database Used for Fertility Histories

The birth-interval method of estimating birth dates requires detailed enumeration of the population from which the fertility histories were formulated. The database contains 519 individuals who have lived in the Mucajai population before or after contact and 32 who were par-ents or siblings of Mucajai people but never entered the population themselves. Four hundred and sixty-three of these have lived in the population at some time since contact. For the reasons indicated in Chapter 1, this represents a perfect or near-perfect enumeration of the postcontact population.

Infanticide raises a question of possible omissions. Such an omission would introduce an error of under 1 year in an estimated fertility his-tory. This is not a large error for estimating birth dates and can be tolerated along with the standard errors. The literature on the Yano-mama has discussed the analytical importance of infanticide and the difficulty of obtaining quantitative data. Chapters 7 and 10 will discuss the known frequency and role of infanticide in the population dynam-ics of this group. Here the methodological question of its enumeration will be discussed. Questions may also arise because of the role of mis-sionaries in the collection of infanticide data.

The birth list kept by the missionaries was informal and the ques-tion of recording infanticides was not raised until the 1970s. During the 1960s the question did not arise because none were known. For this reason the Mucajai group is cited in the literature as having no infanticide (Neel and Weiss, 1975). After his return from Brazil, Pe-ters reviewed the literature with its discussions of infanticide among the Yanomama. He concluded that the Mucajai group must have been concealing them because he had spoken strongly against the practice, especially female infanticide (Peters, 1980).

Nevertheless Peters was never comfortable with this conclusion be-cause he had lived in the village houses and discussed many personal details with individuals which were not concealed even though they knew he did not approve of all of them. If there was an infanticide, the pregnant mother would probably have been noticed by the missionaries.

In the mid-1970s Peters asked his successors at the mission to systematically include infanticides on their list. Twelve were recorded. During the 1970s Peters compiled two censuses and, while doing so, made inquiry about infanticides during the late 1950s and 1960s. Two were reported without difficulty. Both had occurred at times when the regular missionaries were temporarily absent. There did not appear to be any effort at concealment. In verifying the fertility histories formulated for this study, many of them were checked with the mothers themselves or with relatives. Three more were recorded.

The length of the registered birth intervals of the postcontact period can be examined to find out how many could contain an infanticide that was not included in the fertility histories. If an infanticide was not recorded in any way, the mother's fertility history would have a longer-than-expected birth interval between the siblings prior and subsequent to the infanticide. This stretched-out interval would be at least the length of an interval with a stillbirth, 4.1 years (Table 4.4), plus a few more months because it would be a full term. This would total about 4.5 years. Table 4.2 shows that in the postcontact period there are nine regular registered intervals (6.8%) of 4.5 years or longer. There are no exact criteria to evaluate the significance of this figure, but given all the other possible reasons for a longer-than-average birth interval, it does not appear that there is significant omission of infanticides. Some of these longer intervals may contain abortions and stillbirths which were probably underenumerated.

There still remains the possibility of deliberate misreporting of infanticides as due to some other cause or an unknown cause. Such a possibility cannot be entirely eliminated, but this does not appear to be an important consideration. If there was a deliberate attempt at concealment, it is much more likely that the pregnancy would be reported as terminating in an abortion, which it is emically for the Yanomama. It would be easier to do this than to attempt to pass it off as some other type of infant mortality. Again this would result in the stretched-out interval examined above.

A distinction should be made between a certain reticence about such matters as opposed to conspiratorial silence with an active effort to conceal. There is reticence, but deliberate concealment has not been found. The six cases recorded late were due to absences from the mission, people living downstream, and other incidental factors including the Yanomama concept of infanticide as terminal abortion. For these reasons, the authors believe the study has a good enumeration of infanticides.

Some data on infanticides in the precontact period were also obtained, but here the information was clearly deficient. A number of mothers had died prior to verification of the histories. Some were verified with their relatives who may not have been able to know or remember if there were infanticides although some were recorded.

The missionaries never attempted to systematically record abortions although a few were noted. When this research formulated a preliminary version of the fertility histories and Peters checked them with the Mucajai people, most of the information about abortions was obtained. Twenty-eight abortions since contact were retrospectively recorded. This is probably an underenumeration. The data on the number of abortions are the weakest segment of the database.

V. Distinctiveness of the Mucajai Database

The determination of age completes the database. As will be discussed in Chapter 10, there have been few population studies of the Yanomama and other forager/horticultural groups, partly because of the lack of comprehensive demographic data, especially about age. This database overcomes a number of the customary deficiencies. It gives a diachronic picture, as it has a time span of 28 years. It represents a nearly complete, if not a perfect enumeration of all individuals in the postcontact population. It has a high quality of enumeration of the various characteristics of individuals based on a strong ethnographic foundation. Almost 60% of the ages were known from registration, leaving only 40% to be estimated. Data from the 60%, combined with in-depth ethnographic and genealogical data, provided the basis for the estimation methodology. The ethnographic and demographic data are not based on short-term visits or even a year of field work, but have been generated by missionaries who lived in continuous contact with the Mucajai group. These qualities indicate the reliability of the data for analyzing the population dynamics of the Mucajai Yanomama.

Six

Migration

Net migration is the result of in-migration and out-migration. This chapter first analyzes in-migration which, together with fertility, causes population increase. It then considers out-migration, a variable contributing to population decrease. Finally, the question of the significance of migration in the population dynamics is examined.

I. History of Contacts with Other Yanomama Groups in the Postcontact Period

Migration is usually dependent on previous contacts with other Yanomama groups who are either its sources or recipients. Between the Maquiritare wars in the 1930s and the arrival of the missionaries, the Mucajai group was isolated from all Yanomama and non-Yanomama. Consequently there had been no in-migration or out-migration during this period. The following is a brief history of the contacts between the Mucajai and other Yanomama groups in the postcontact period and the subsequent in-migration from each group (Table 6.1). Refer

Table 6.1

In-Migration and Out-Migration by Group and Reason for Out-Migration[a]

Group	First contact		Reason						Out-migration	Net migration
	Year	How	Marry	Captive	Refuge	Other	Sum	%		
Precontact										
Wehe	?	?		1			1			
Maku	?	?		1			1			
Maquiritare	?	?		3			3			
Total				5			5			
Postcontact										
Marashiteri	1959	Miners	10		1	1	12	20.7	4	8
Shiriteri	1959	Marash.		3			3	5.2		3
Aica	1959	Miss.	10			3	13	22.4	1	12
Xiriana	1960	Miss.			2		2	3.4	1	1
Paramiteri	1960	Miss.	7		10	1	18	31.0	1	17
Catrimani	1961	Miss.		8		1	9	15.5		9
Maku	none	none	1				1	1.7		1
Total			28	11	13	6	58	100	7	51
%			48.3	19.0	22.4	10.3		100		
Missionaries			17	8	12	5	42			
% of reason			60.7	72.7	92.3	83.3	72.4			

[a]Abbreviations: Marash., Marashiteri; Miss., missionaries.

to the map inside the front and back covers for the approximate location of these groups.

A. Marashiteri

Early in 1959 two Brazilian mining prospectors passed through the area and ascended the Mucajai River. Upon their return, they brought information that the Marashiteri lived upstream. At that time the Kaserapai were dying from infectious disease acquired on downstream trips. To explain this sickness and death, they initially speculated that they resulted from Marashiteri witchcraft. They journeyed upstream to confront this village of about 80 people, but the Marashiteri persuaded them that the witchcraft emanated from the Shiriteri. Friendly relationships developed between the Mucajai and Marashiteri villagers and marriage exchange began in 1966. Twenty-one percent of the in-migrants came from this group.

B. Shiriteri

This small group lived in the mountains a 7-day journey to the west from the Mucajai. The first contact was a raid in 1959 by the Mucajai group in conjunction with the Marashiteri. Five percent of the in-migration has come from this group.

C. Aica

This group was first contacted in April 1959 when some men from the Mucajai group accompanied the missionaries on a survey trip. They lived 6 days by trail to the southeast on the Apiau River. At that time there were only two small villages of 16 and 24 people. They had suffered high mortality due to diseases contracted from Brazilian rubber tappers. Intermarriage began in 1960 and over the years Aica have continued to marry into the Mucajai group. Twenty-two percent of the in-migration has been from this group.

D. Paramiteri

This group lived on the Uraricuera River, a trail journey of 5 days to the north and 2 days west by canoe. The first mission station of the Unevangelized Fields Mission was founded among them in the spring of 1958. The Brazilian Air Force requested that the missionaries lengthen their airstrip. In 1960 Peters and four single Mucajai men flew there to help with the work. Marriage exchange began in 1968.

Thirty-one percent of the in-migrants come from this group, the largest amount from any one group.

E. Xiriana

This group lived an arduous 10-day overland trip to the north on the Uraricaa River and the headwaters of the Paragua River in Venezuela. The Mucajai people heard about the Xiriana from the missionaries for the first time since they had fissioned more than 30 years previously. The linguist, Migliazza, informed the missionaries that there were relatives of the Mucajai group among the Xiriana. This information was later confirmed by the Paramiteri who were in frequent contact with the Xiriana. Some Paramiteri accompanied a Xiriana group on a visit to the Mucajai villages in 1961. Groups from Mucajai have visited the Xiriana two or three times since then. They seldom see each other because of the difficult journey and because the Xiriana have their own sources of trade goods. Three percent of the in-migrants come from this group.

F. Catrimani

This group lived an 8-day journey to the southeast of the Mucajai people on the Catrimani River. The first contact was made in 1961 by some Mucajai men who accompanied the missionaries on a survey trip. News of this group continued to reach the Mucajai group through the Aica, who had established marital ties with both groups. Sixteen percent of the in-migrants come from this group.

II. Reasons for In-migration

The main reasons for in-migrating to the Mucajai group are marriage, as captives seized in raids, and flight from one's native village to avoid revenge.

A. Marriage

Almost half the in-migrants entered the Mucajai population for marriage. They include 19 adults (6 men and 13 women of whom 4 were widows finding remarriage difficult in their own villages) and 9 children who came with the 4 widows. For Mucajai men, the reason for seeking outside marriage was the lack of females within the group with the correct kinship status. Some men had wife-sharing arrangements as secondary husbands but wanted marriage as primary husbands. In two of the marriages Mucajai and Paramiteri men exchanged their sisters. One woman was stolen from her Paramiteri family by a Mucajai man. All 13 new wives came to live in the Mucajai community without the Mucajai men spending several years of bride service with the bride's family. The Mucajai men preferred to remain in their own villages with their kin and not to be burdened with the mother-in-law avoidance patterns. The families of the wives agreed to a short period of bride service because of the trade goods the Mucajai men were able to provide them and because of the prestige of the Mucajai group. In addition, medical assistance was available at Mucajai. The Mucajai people were known as an industrious group who were willing to work hard and to provide for their families, while some other groups had a reputation for laziness. During the postcontact period, no Mucajai male has out-migrated for marriage.

B. Women Captured in Raids

Forced in-migration applies to 11 women and their children seized when Mucajai men raided other Yanomama groups. At the time of contact there were five captive women in the population. In the postcontact period, Mucajai groups have been involved in four raids against other Yanomama groups. In 1959 there was much infectious disease. The resulting sickness and death was a new and frightening experience for the Mucajai community. In their efforts to explain what was happening, the Mucajai asked the Marashiteri. The Marashiteri said that the Shiriteri were performing witchcraft against the Mucajai. Since the Mucajai people had no contact with the Shiriteri and did not consider them enemies, they visited them to get an explanation. The Marashiteri acted as guides. The Marashiteri then warned the Shiriteri about hostile intentions of the Mucajai people, even though the Mucajai had not yet made any judgments about the Shiriteri. It appears that the Marashiteri were manipulating both groups for their own unknown purposes. When the Shiriteri showed themselves suspicious and reserved toward the Mucajai group and refused to give the customary offerings of food for visitors, the Mucajai people saw this as proof of the accusations made by the Marashiteri. The two visiting groups, the Mucajai and the Marashiteri, changed into a raiding party and attacked the Shiriteri. One Shiriteri was shot with a gun, one was killed by his own knife, and two were mortally stabbed with bamboo arrow tips. The Mucajai took three women captives and the Marashiteri seized two. Years later the Mucajai sent presents to the surviving Shiriteri relatives of their captive wives as a goodwill gesture.

In 1968 Mucajai men raided a group living on the Catrimani River. In a Mucajai village a woman had died suddenly. Later a Catrimani man visited the village and said that he was responsible for the witchcraft which had killed her. He also insulted the Mucajai group by saying they were "not fierce." These events inflamed an already existing animosity against the Catrimani. The Aica brother-in-law of a prominent Mucajai man had been killed in a raid by the Catrimani. The Mucajai group sought revenge for the witchcraft death, for the death of the brother-in-law, and for the insults. With the help of an Aica guide, the raiding party made its way to the Catrimani River. There they were well received by the Catrimani, who gave them welcoming gifts of meat and bananas. They thought the Mucajai group had come for a friendly visit. On the third day the shooting, stabbing, axing, and stoning began. In a short period of time, eight Catrimani men were killed. Four women aged 16, 17, 19, and 20 were seized as captives along with four of their children ranging in ages from one to seven.

Small groups of Mucajai men participated in two other raids. In 1970 they helped the Marashiteri raid the Duhunteri to avenge sickness due to witchcraft. In 1978 they helped the Paramiteri raid the Parahudi for the same reason. In both cases, the Mucajai men had inmigrant wives from the raiding groups and they were fulfilling their obligations of reciprocity. No women captives were taken by the Mucajai in either of these raids.

C. In-migrants Seeking Refuge

Several family groups and single individuals have moved to the Mucajai villages following killings and disputes in their own villages. Two male heads of families had killed fellow villagers, one in a drunken brawl and the other in an argument. To escape the expected revenge by the families of the deceased, these men and their families fled.

D. Other In-Migration

Six people have in-migrated for other reasons. Some came to be with relatives who had in-migrated earlier. One was a Catrimani infant who had been abandoned by his parents and adopted by a Mucajai couple.

III. Out-Migration

There have been seven out-migrants in the postcontact period. All of these were previous in-migrants and all out-migrated in the third phase. Five returned to their original villages. Some left because of bad marriages; others were widows who decided to return to their own people; two left to marry among their original people. (There were also two sisters who were born in a Mucajai village and later left. They married, lived for several years among the Aica, and then returned with their husbands and children. Technically they are out-migrants and in-migrants, but since the number is insignificant, these two

Table 6.2

Rates of In-Migration and Out-Migration per 1000 Population[a]

		In-migration			
Age rates		Phases			
Sex	Age	1	2	3	Total
M	0	29	4	3	9
F	0	27	6	7	12
M	15	7	4	19	10
F	15	65	16	4	25
M	30	4	10	11	8
F	30	60	15		18
M	45	—	—	—	—
F	45		10		3
Crude rates					
In-migration		24.2	5.7	5.8	10.4
Out-migration				3.3	1.4
Net migration		24.2	5.7	2.5	9.0

[a]The Mucajai population forms the denominators of all rates of migration.

women have not been counted as migrants although they were re-
moved from the population count for the periods in which they were
absent. The husbands of both and the children of one are considered
in-migrants for marriage. The other woman is the single case of permanent sterility previously mentioned.)

IV. Net Migration

Net migration has been a significant factor in the increase of the Mucajai population. Table 6.2 shows that this was primarily due to in-
migration and that it was especially significant in the first phase as
indicated by the 24.2 crude rate, or 34 individuals added to the existing population.

The in-migration was highly age selective. The highest age-specific
rates (Table 6.2) of the postcontact period were in phase 1 for the
female reproductive population. Since these rates are spread over the
11 years comprising phase 1, they do not show the sharp impact of
the in-migration in the individual years in which it took place. In
1960 there were two women in the 15 to 29 age group who in-migrated to join six existing women of these ages. Also two women in
the 30 to 44 age group entered to join five existing women of like
ages. The in-migration rates were 333 and 400 (per 1000 population),
respectively, for these age groups in this single year. In 1968, 5 women
captives from the Catrimani raid between the ages of 15 and 29 joined
the 18 resident women of the same age bracket for an age-specific rate
of 277. The in-migration added to the female reproductive population
in greater proportion than any other age–sex group.

Out-migration was so slight that no age-specific rates were calculated. The impact of the 24 male and 34 female in-migrants is mitigated by the 1 male and 6 female out-migrants, all of whom were
previously in-migrants. However for later analysis, the important
question is: Are the out-migrant females in the reproductive age
group? Five fall into this category, one in her late teens who was child-
less at the time and four in their twenties. These latter four had ten
children during their residence among the Mucajai, and all remained
at the time of their mother's out-migration. Therefore their out-migration did not completely nullify the reproductive effects of their in-
migration.

Seven

Mortality

At death the bodies are carried to the woods where they remain for several months until the flesh decays. The bones are then burned and pulverized into ashes which are collected in two gourds. These are buried beneath the hammock of a female relative. Later, at large feasts, the gourds are unearthed and the ashes are smeared on the bodies of the men and children. These activities signify respect for the dead and fear of punishment if they are not performed.

Table 7.1 shows the distribution of the 129 postcontact deaths by age, sex, and cause for the three phases. The analysis of cause of death in this chapter and its variation between phases is hindered by lack of biological data. There were no laboratory facilities at the Mucajai dispensary for diagnostic purposes, nor have any biological studies been done on the Mucajai population. A small percentage of cases were diagnosed in Boa Vista, but for most deaths from natural causes there are only the impressions of the missionaries. There were a number of deaths preceded by morbidity with fevers, colds, and diarrhea. The missionaries classified these cases as malaria, pneumonia, measles, whooping cough, diarrhea, dysentery, or tuberculosis. Here they have been grouped together in a general category called infectious

Table 7.1
Number of Deaths by Age, Sex and Phase, and Cause[a]

| | | Phases | | | | | | Totals | | |
| | | 1 | | 2 | | 3 | | | Reason | Reason |
Cause	Age	M	F	M	F	M	F	Total	total	%
	0	5	7	7	13	18	17	67		
	15	8	6	1	2	3	2	22		
	30	9	2	0	0	0	0	11		
	45+	10	6	1	1	8	6	32		
	Total	32	21	9	16	29	25	132		
	%	60.3	39.6	36	64	53.7	46.3			
	Total	53		25		54		132		
	%	40.2		18.9		40.9				100
Infectious disease	0	2	2	4	4	11	7	30		
	15	3	3		2	2	1	11		
	30	5	1					6		
	45+	5	3	1		4	3	16	63	47.0
Infanticide	0	1	3	1	5	3	5	18	18	13.6
Other known	0	1	1	2		1		5		
	15	4	1			1	1	7		
	30	2	1					3		
	45+					1		1	16	12.1
Unknown	0	1	1		4	3	5	14		
	15	1	2	1				4		
	30	2						2		
	45+	5	3		1	3	3	15	35	27.2
Total		32	21	9	16	29	25	132	132	

[a]Two deaths between 11/9/58 and 12/31/58 dropped in rate calculations.

diseases and comprise almost half of all the deaths. Fourteen percent of the deaths were infanticides. Twelve percent were cases of other known causes including five homicides and two cases of food poisonings, and the remainder were a variety of causes, each of which was responsible for a single death. For 28% of the deaths there was no known cause. If one assumes no systematic cause for the unknown cases, then the percentage distribution of known cases is representative of the distribution for all cases. The validity of this assumption is unknown, but the category may be analytically helpful and is used in

Table 7.2
Mortality Rates: Years of Life Expectancy, Probability of Dying Per 1000 Population, Percentage Survivorship, Crude Death per 1000 Population[a]

	Phases					Sex	
Rate	1	2	3	Total	n	M	F
Average individual, years life expectancy, e_0	32.8	55.1	39.1	38.9		38.5	40.5
Age probability							
q 0 age	133	79	210	140	36	118	163
1	43	89	123	92	20	51	139
5	62	46	14	35	6	56	12
10	61		81	45	6	51	48
20	392	84	105	190	18	225	152
30	365			114	8	136	78
40	277		116	139	7	193	—
50	645	148	205	323	11	357	256
60	862		506	485	9	571	408
70 +	1000	1000	1000	1000	6	1000	1000
n	51	25	54	130	130	69	61
% Age survivorship							
l 0 age	100	100	100	100		100	100
1	87	92	79	86		88	83
10	78	80	68	75		79	71
30	45	73	56	58		59	57
50	20	73	39	44		42	53
Group mortality Crude rate	36.3	12.3	26.0	23.4			

[a]Life table calculations: $q(0-1)$ = deaths $0-1$/births
$q(x)$ = $2n * M(x.n) / 2 + n M(x.n)$
No further adjustments were made.

the tables. Table 7.2 presents mortality rates for each of the three analytical levels, and Fig. 7.1 graphs the annual rates of group mortality.

I. Infectious Disease

Infectious diseases are the principal cause of mortality in all three phases. The differing levels of mortality between the three phases are mainly due to their variation and the variation of the unknown cases,

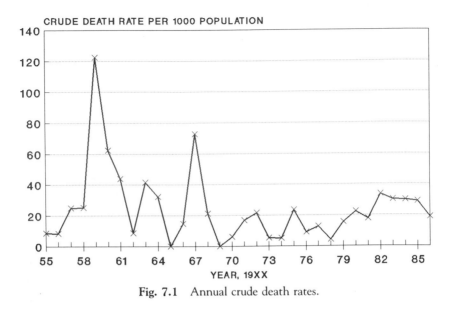

Fig. 7.1 Annual crude death rates.

some of which were probably additional infectious disease. The Mucajai group experienced sudden and high mortality from infectious disease shortly before permanent contact. In the first phase of the postcontact period (1959–1969), 22 of the 50 deaths (44%) were due to such diseases. During the two downstream trips to obtain steel tools, 13 months and 2 months prior to permanent contact, the Mucajai contracted respiratory infections from the Brazilians and many died after they returned upstream. They had no immunity due to their previous isolation. The missionaries arrived during a high mortality crisis. They had been aware of the danger of infectious disease among previously unexposed groups before coming upstream. All mission personnel went through a period of quarantine prior to coming to the Mucajai group and the program has been continued for all three phases.

During the first phase the missionaries initiated their medical program. They dispensed medicines. Three serious medical cases were sent to Boa Vista for treatment and one infant received an operation in Rio de Janeiro. Preventive measures were taken. In 1966 a Brazilian physician immunized the group against tuberculosis. Spraying to prevent malaria was initiated about the same time.

Contacts with the outside world were limited. The missionaries introduced the Mucajai to other Yanomama groups. The Mucajai men who sought wives from these groups would spend some months away from the village while performing a short term of service for their bride's parents. These other Yanomama groups were also relatively isolated. The only visitors from the national society were Brazilian government personnel representing the Indian Protective Service (later called FUNAI) and the Air Force. The Mucajai made about two downstream trips a year during this period to trade canoes and short-term labor to Brazilian frontiersmen for knives, machetes, pots, and clothing.

The infectious diseases of phase 1 primarily affected adults 20 years of age and older as indicated by the elevated age-specific rates in Table 7.2. The mortality rate was extremely high for those in their twenties, who composed the majority of those making the downstream trips. Mortality remained relatively high for those in their thirties and then soared at age forty so that the rates are distinctly elevated above those for the other two phases. Adults age 20 and up comprise 82% of the infectious disease in this phase. The diseases had little impact on infants and children. The reason for this is unknown since the types of infectious disease are not certain.

The middle phase (1970–1979) had low mortality even though infectious disease still accounted for 42% of the deaths. Several reasons appear important for the low mortality of this phase. The Mucajai group probably acquired some natural immunity to these diseases so that their effect was not as lethal as in the previous phase. The clinical and preventive efforts of the medical program were probably having an impact. These efforts were increased during this phase and more cases were referred to Brazilian medical services in Boa Vista. The immunization efforts were expanded to include diphtheria–whooping cough–tetanus, measles, yellow fever, and tuberculosis. The immunization program was continuous and records were kept to ensure its effectiveness. Contact with the national society was still limited compared with the events of the third phase. A few Mucajai performed wage labor downstream at an isolated Brazilian ranch. The downstream trips continued with the Mucajai remaining away from the villages for longer periods than in phase 1. FUNAI hired two Mucajai men to work in the pacification of other Yanomama areas.

In the third phase overall mortality rose and 28 of the 53 deaths

(53%) were from infectious disease. The age-specific rates indicate that the age structure of infectious disease also shifted so that its impact was much greater on infants and children and less on those in the upper ages than in phase 1. Fifty-seven percent of the infectious disease mortality was among infants-children and only 29% was among adults age 20 and over. The reason for this shift is unknown because of the lack of biological data.

The increase of infectious disease in the third phase appears related to increased contact with the national society and other Yanomama groups who, in turn, have increased their contacts with the national society. Much of the increased contact is the result of gold mining by the Mucajai people in their traditional areas. A Shiriana taught them how to build sluices and the Marashiteri, after observing Brazilian miners, taught their Mucajai kin how to pan for gold. A number of men have found gold and sell it for cash in Boa Vista, the regional capitol of the Roraima District. Trips for this purpose have led to increased interaction with Brazilian agriculturists, traders, government personnel, and many others. This has exposed the Mucajai to the complete spectrum of infectious diseases in the rural Brazilian population. The acquisition of two outboard motors has also increased their facility to travel. Radios, sewing machines, and Brazilian clothing have become part of Mucajai life in this phase.

II. Induced Abortion and Infanticide

Sometimes death immediately follows birth. Infanticide is one of the reasons. Induced abortion is also discussed here because it results from the same set of circumstances as infanticide. The Yanomama define infanticides as terminal abortions. (In demographic convention, abortion is a fetal rather than a demographic mortality because it is not preceded by a birth.) The techniques of abortion and infanticide will be described, then the reasons for their use.

An induced abortion takes place as soon as the fetus can be grasped from outside the body by pushing with the hands into the abdomen. This occurs at the end of the second month or early in the third month of pregnancy. The abortion is usually performed by the woman's husband or by her mother or mother-in-law, or if no one else is available, by the woman herself. As preparation, the pregnant woman eats little for 2 or 3 days prior to the abortion. This empties the alimentary organs, which facilitates locating the fetus. The pregnant woman lies in her hammock. The abortionist warms his or her knuckles over the fire. Then they push inward and upward on the woman's abdomen searching for the fetus. When it is located, it is crushed with both hands. The abortion is usually accompanied by great pain. The procedure may be repeated on two succeeding evenings. The fetus along with much blood passes 12 hours to 3 days afterward.

Infanticides usually occur immediately after the birth. When the newborn slides onto the banana leaves laid on the ground, it is not nurtured in any way. Usually the father or one of the grandmothers chokes the newborn by standing on the ends of a stick placed across its throat. Sometimes it will be smothered.

Table 7.3 shows that the most important reason for abortion is protection of the nursling as described in Chapter 4. This accounts for 32% of all cases and 40% of cases where the reason is known. Women who become pregnant when they have no husbands account for 14%. All of these women were widowed or separated. This means there is no man to provide the meat considered necessary for the child's development. The case of a pregnancy before a girl is physically ready for motherhood was described in Chapter 4. Marital conflict may precipitate abortion. A woman may believe that her husband plans to leave her and will not provide meat for the child. Abortion may be performed to spite the husband for whatever reason the conflict may have originated. Perceived deformity is also a cause of abortion. If it

Table 7.3
Frequency of and Reasons for Induced Abortion and Infanticide

Reason	Abortion			Infanticide		
	No.	%	% Known	n	%	% Known
Protect nursling	9	32.1	40.1	2	11.8	13.3
Deformity	1	3.6	4.5	3	17.6	20.0
Female too young	3	10.7	13.6	1	5.9	6.7
Too many girls				3	17.6	20.0
No husband	4	14.3	18.2	4	23.5	26.7
Husband not father	2	7.1	9.0	1	5.9	6.7
Marital conflict	3	10.7	13.6	1	5.9	6.7
Unknown	6	21.4	X	2	11.8	X
Total	28	100	100	17	100	100

is believed that something is wrong with the fetus from the progress of the pregnancy, an abortion is performed to prevent the birth of a deformed child.

The reasons for infanticide are much the same as for abortion. The two most important causes are preferential female infanticide (too many girls relative to the number of boys) and widowed or separated women without husbands. These together account for about 50% of the infanticides. Preferential female infanticide means that while infants of both sexes become victims of infanticide, there are occasions when it is done only because the infant is female. Male domination is a strong characteristic of Yanomama culture as shown by the autobiographical account of Helena Valero (Valero, 1984), the ethnographic accounts of Cocco (1972) and Chagnon (1977), and field experience among the Mucajai group. Females are the property of their primary husbands and become pawns in male kinship arrangements for political and economic purposes. For these reasons, a male is desired as the first child. If the first child is female, it may (but not necessarily) be killed to hasten another pregnancy, hopefully a male. Likewise, if a woman gives birth to two or three females in a row or if the primary husband feels he already has enough daughters from other wives, the female infant may be killed so that another pregnancy, again hopefully a male, can take place.

Since the sex of an infant and most deformities are not known until birth, infanticide will be practiced rather than abortion. The deformity may be insignificant by contemporary medical standards. Valero (1984) cites a case of webbed fingers. The Yanomama fear any physical handicap and the ridicule that invariably accompanies it. It is not known why the remaining cases became infanticides rather than abortions. Perhaps a woman was hoping for a better relationship with the father that did not materialize. Or the proper time for an abortion may have passed without a decision.

III. Infant Mortality

Infant mortality rates have a volatile range, from 79 to 210. In the postcontact period, there were 17 infant deaths from infanticide, 14 from infectious disease, and 7 from other or unknown causes, some of which probably were infectious disease. Therefore infanticide and

Table 7.4

Impact of Infanticide on Infant Mortality and Crude Death Rates per 1000 Population

	Phase			
Mortality rate	1	2	3	Total
Infant rates				
Infant mortality (IM)	133	79	210	140
Infanticide	50	53	76	61
Other infant	83	26	134	79
% Infanticide of IM	37.5	66.6	36.3	43.6
Crude death rates				
Crude death (CDR)	36.3	12.3	26.0	23.4
Crude infanticide	2.1	2.8	3.9	3.0
Other crude death	34.2	9.5	22.1	20.4
% Infanticide of CDR	5.8	22.8	15.0	13.0

infectious diseases are the most important causes in the structure of the infant death rate. Table 7.4 shows the mortality rates for infanticide alone and for other causes. Infanticides add about 3 per 1000 to the group crude rate. They heavily affect the infant death rates. Without them, these rates decline to 83 and 25 (per 1000 population) in the first two phases. This indicates that the infant death rate from natural causes for this type of population is relatively low compared to some other populations.

The high infant mortality of the third phase represents an increase in infectious disease and an increase in the number of infanticides. Two of the infanticides involved mothers with no husbands, three because of deformities, one because the mother was too young, and one for an unknown reason. They appear to result from the traditional cultural factors calling for infanticide and do not suggest any systemic factor related to the cultural changes of the third phase.

IV. Other Causes of Death

There have been five homicides in the postcontact period. All the victims were male. Two young men went to visit the Xiriana and never returned. The Xiriana claimed they arrived and departed, but the Mucajai people have always felt they were killed by the Xiriana and this judgment is used in the classification. Another was killed when he encountered a Yanomama hunting band and was pierced by an arrow after he had killed several of the band. Another homicide occurred when a young Aica immigrant irritated an older one who shot him. There have been two female deaths from inadvertent consumption of toxic foods. There are no reported cases of maternal deaths.

V. Yanomama Perception of Cause of Death

The Yanomama do not have an elaborate system of disease classification. Usually symptoms are described and it is implied that the death resulted from these symptoms in some unspecified manner. However there is an emic category used to explain mortality which will become an important factor in the analysis of the overall population dynamics—witchcraft. When the high mortality from infectious disease began to occur, the Mucajai were extremely upset and wanted an explanation. The deaths were perceived to be the result of witchcraft by other Yanomama villages. When mortalities are interpreted in this way, there may be an ensuing raid of revenge on the bewitching village. This perception of witchcraft was responsible for all four raids in which the Mucajai group have been involved in the postcontact period as well as the in-migration resulting from them.

VI. Life Expectancy and Group Mortality

Table 7.2 shows age-specific probabilities of death. The mortality of the average individual is expressed by the e_0 function of the life table called life expectancy at birth. The Mucajai expectancy fluctuates between 32.8 and 55.1 years. These life expectancy figures should be considered only as indicators of the force of mortality expressed by the age schedules from which they were derived. They are not accurate predictors of the duration of life of the individuals comprising the synthetic cohort because of the small numbers, migration, and volatility of the mortality structure as well as the overall demographic volatility of this type of population.

Table 7.2 also examines sex differences in mortality. Gender does not discriminate life expectancy. No significance can be attributed to the small difference because of the small number of deaths (69 males and 61 females, one unknown sex of an infanticide). The higher mortality rate for females 1 to 4 years of age raises the possibility of neglect of infant females for the same reasons as preferential female infanticide. However the missionaries have never noticed neglect of female infants. Some of the difference between this and the male rate is probably due to the volatility of small numbers (6 male and 14 female deaths between these ages in the postcontact period).

The crude rates indicate the levels of group mortality. Figure 7.1 graphs them for each individual year and indicates the high volatility of mortality. The peak in 1959 and the lesser continuation in 1960 result from the respiratory infections acquired on the downstream trips. The 1967 peak is due to measles and whooping cough. The 1963 peak is primarily due to a year of average mortality increased by the two presumed homicides by the Xiriana. When grouped by phases the crude rates remain volatile with a range of 11.9 to 36.3.

PART THREE

Synthesis

Eight

How the Population Increased

This chapter synthesizes the previous chapters to explain how the Mucajai population increased from 121 people at the time of first permanent contact in 1958 to 319 at the beginning of 1987, an increase of 198 people or an annual average of 3.5% in over 28 years. This high rate of increase is unusual considering the sexual imbalance at the time of contact. Females comprised only 22.6% of the 15- to -44 age group. The increase resulted both from the direct contributions of the demographic variables and from their indirect contribution through their effect on the age–sex structure of the population. This chapter examines these relationships and in so doing reveals the importance of certain cultural factors for the increase.

I. Components of Total Increase

Table 8.1 shows the absolute and relative contributions of the demographic variables. Figures 8.1 through 8.4 plot the rates and their interrelationships for the individual years to give a synoptic view. Figure 8.1 shows the relationships between the annual fertility and mortality

Table 8.1

Frequencies and Rates of the Demographic Variables in the Postcontact Period

Contact 11/9/58	Demographic variables	Postcontact							End 1/1/87
		Phases				Total			
		1	2	3	Total	Total	M	F	
Population 121	Births	60	114	105	279	279	144	135	Population 319
M 77	Deaths	52	26	54	132	132	69	63	M 175
F 44	Natural Increase	7	89	51	147	147	75	72	F 144
%F 36.4	In-migration	34	12	12	58	58	24	34	%F 45.1
	Out-migration	—	—	7	7	7	1	6	
	Net migration	34	12	5	51	51	23	28	
	Total increase	41	101	55	198	198	98	100	
	Crude Rates						%F		
	Birth	40.0	54.1	50.6		49.9	48.4		
	Death	36.3	12.3	26.0		23.3	47.7		
	Natural Increase	4.7	41.8	24.6		26.6	49.0		
	In-migration	24.2	5.7	5.8		10.4	58.6		
	Out-migration	—	—	3.9		1.4	85.7		
	Net migration	24.2	5.7	1.9		9.0	54.9		
	Total increase	28.9	47.5	26.5		35.6	50.5		

rates that result in natural increase (represented by the area between the two on the graph). Its exact values are shown in Fig. 8.3. There was high group fertility in all three phases. It increased between phases 1 and 2 but, as shown by the relative constancy of the total fertility rate in Chapter 4, this is due to changes in the age–sex structure of the population, not fertility itself. The balanced sex ratio at birth (51.6%) contributed to correcting the sexual imbalance found at the time of contact.

The 129 deaths were distributed in a highly variable manner, not only annually as shown in Fig. 8.1, but also among the phases. In the first phase infectious disease elevated mortality to higher levels than fertility in four of the years. The positive areas (natural increase) between the birth and death lines almost cancel out the negative areas (natural decrease). Fertility fluctuates in its usual manner, but because of infectious disease there is almost no natural increase. This may be typical of the initial contact period for a previously isolated group. Once some natural immunity is acquired and immunization programs are initiated, mortality drops dramatically in phase 2 as shown in Fig. 8.1. It rises again in phase 3 due to increased infectious disease.

Figure 8.2 shows the interrelationship of the annual in-migration and out-migration rates that result in net migration (the area between the two in this figure). The exact values are shown in Fig. 8.3. Since out-migration is zero in most years, it falls along the bottom axis of the graph. Fifty-eight people entered the population as in-migrants and seven of these later left. The rate of in-migration in the first phase was one-half of the fertility level for the same period. If it had not been for this high level of in-migration from captives and people coming for marriage, the mortality losses (53 per 1000 population) would have almost offset the increase from fertility (60 per 1000).

In the postcontact period, natural increase accounted for three-fourths of the total increase and net migration for one-fourth (Table 8.1, Fig. 8.3). The rate of total increase is shown in Fig. 8.4. Females constituted 50.5% of the total increase. The 198 net total increase added to the 121 population at the time of contact gives the 319 population at the beginning of 1987 (Fig. 3.1). (Figures 8.4 and 3.1 show essentially the same thing. There is a slight difference in the graphs because Fig. 3.1 is based on Table 3.1, which employs beginning-of-the-year populations. Figure 8.4 is based on crude rates, which employ middle-of-the-year populations.)

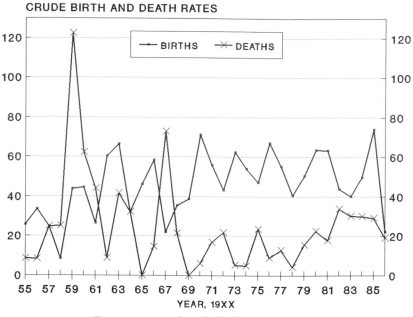

Fig. 8.1 Annual crude birth and death rates.

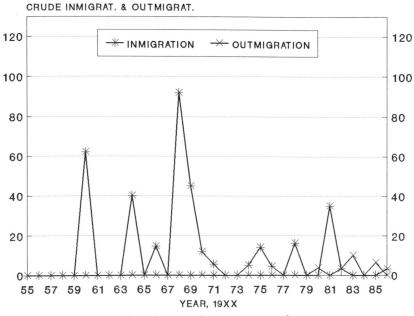

Fig. 8.2 Annual crude rates of in-migration and out-migration.

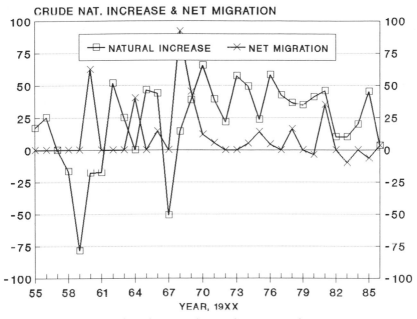

Fig. 8.3   Annual crude rates of natural increase and net migration.

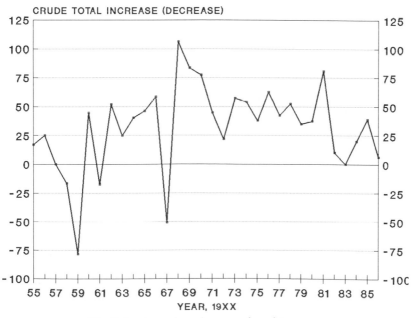

Fig. 8.4   Annual crude rates of total increase.

II. Change of Age–Sex Structure of the Population

During the postcontact period the Mucajai population not only grew in size, but its age–sex structure changed (Fig. 8.5). The female proportion of the population increased from 36.4 to 44.6% as indicated in Table 8.2. The population grew younger as indicated by the decline of 9 years in the median age and by the increase of the proportion ages 0–14 constitute of the total population.

These changes in the age–sex structure caused changes in the levels of fertility. Females of reproductive age increased their proportion of the population by 9.5% (from 11.6 to 21.1%) as shown in Table 8.2 and Fig. 8.5. This means that even though average fertility per female (total fertility rate) declined slightly, group fertility increased.

Table 8.2
Change of Age–Sex Structure in the Postcontact Period

Age	Total	Male	Female	% Male	% Female	%d
			Contact population			
0	37	19	18	15.7	14.9	+ .8
15	62	48	14	39.7	11.6	+ 28.1
45+	22	10	12	8.3	9.9	− 1.6
Total	121	77	44	63.7	36.4	+ 27.3
Median	24.6	18.2	27.2			
			Population at 1/1/87			
Age	Total	Male	Female	% Male	% Female	%d
0	156	90	66	28.6	20.4	+ 7.8
15	127	59	68	18.5	21.1	− 2.8
45+	36	26	10	8.2	3.1	+ 5.1
Total	319	175	144	55.3	44.6	+ 9.8
Median	15.6	16.8	14.4			
			Change (contact - 1987)			
Age	Total	Male	Female	% Male	% Female	
0	119	72	48	+ 12.9	+ 5.5	
15	65	11	54	− 21.2	+ 9.5	
45+	14	16	− 2	− .1	− 6.8	
Total	198	98	100	− 8.3	+ 8.3	
Median	− 9.0	− 1.4	− 12.8			

"%d, percent difference.

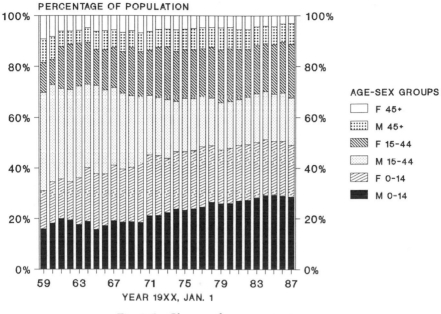

PERCENTAGE OF POPULATION

AGE-SEX GROUPS

- ☐ F 45+
- ▦ M 45+
- ▨ F 15-44
- ▧ M 15-44
- ▨ F 0-14
- ■ M 0-14

YEAR 19XX, JAN. 1

Fig. 8.5 Change of age–sex structure.

The changes in the age structure also helped to lower group mortality between phases 1 and 2. Due to the heavy mortality in phase 1 among the 20-year-old males and those in their 50s and 60s of both sexes, there were proportionately fewer older people in the population than previously and more in the 2–14 age categories, which have lower probabilities of death.

III. In-Migration as a Key Factor of Change

In-migration was an important cause of change in the Mucajai demographic structure. Its direct contribution can be seen in Table 8.1, where its absolute and relative values (crude rate of in-migration) are shown. If crude rates were being used in this study with the simplifying assumption of constancy of age–sex structure, this would express the total contribution of in-migration. This assumption cannot be used, as noted in Chapter 3.

Eighty-one percent of the in-migrants were under 30 years of age. This helped to make the population younger as indicated by the decline in the median age, especially for females. In-migration helped to change the sex structure because almost 60% of the in-migrants were female. Even more important was the change in the sexual proportions of the reproductive ages. Females comprised 68.2% of the in-migrants between the ages of 15 and 44 (Table 8.3). This along with a balanced sex ratio at birth (107 or 51.6%), nearly doubled the percentage the female reproductive population comprised of the total population, from 11.6 to 21.1%, as shown in Table 8.2 and Fig. 8.5.

Table 8.3
In-Migration and Out-Migration by Age, Sex, and Phase; Reason for In-Migration

Reason for In-migration	Age	Phase 1 M	Phase 1 F	Phase 2 M	Phase 2 F	Phase 3 M	Phase 3 F	Total	Total M	F	%F	%F
	0	8	8	2	2	2	3	25	12	13	52.0	
	15	2	11	1	3	4	1	22	7	15	68.2	
	30+	1	4	2	2	2	—	11	5	6	54.5	
	Total	11	23	5	7	8	4	58	24	34	58.6	
	%	19	40	9	12	14	7	100				
Marriage	0	5	5	2				12	5	7	58.3	
	15	2	7	1	2			12	3	9	75.0	
	30+	1		1	1	1		4	3	1	25.0	60.7
Captives	0	2	2					4	2	2	50.0	
	15		6					6		6	100.0	
	30+		1					1		1	100.0	81.8
Refuge	0	1				2	3	6	3	3	50.0	
	15				1	3	1	5	3	2	40.0	
	30+			1		1		2	2		0.0	38.5
Other	0			2	1			3	2	1	33.3	
	15				1	1		2	1	1	50.0	
	30+		1					1		1	100.0	50.0
Total		11	23	5	7	8	4	58	24	34	58.6	58.6
Total			34		12		12	58				
%			58.6		12.6		12.6	100				
Out-migration	0											
	15					1	3	4	1	3	75.0	
	30											
	45+						3	3		3	100.0	
Total						1	6	7	1	6	85.7	
%						17	86	100				

This increase in the female reproductive population had further de-mographic consequences. The in-migrant women of reproductive ages either began or continued childbearing according to the reproductive pattern described in Chapter 4. In-migration, therefore, not only added the in-migrants themselves to the population, but was a factor for their children born after in-migration.

This increase of fertility had a further effect in changing the age–sex structure. Fertility adds people to an age–sex distribution at only one age, age 0, rather than over the entire age distribution. Therefore, all other factors remaining equal, the rise in fertility brings about a rise in the proportion of the population in the 0 age classification each year relative to the other age classifications. Table 8.2 shows an 18.2% increase between contact and 1987 in the 0–14 classification. In-migration through its effect on fertility was responsible for a sig-nificant portion of this change. It was also due to fertility remaining high in phase 1 while mortality was concentrated above 20 years of age.

IV. Raiding and the Sex Ratio

Were the cultural factors responsible for in-migration emically per-ceived and consciously used by the Yanomama to alter the sex ratio? Specifically, are raids conducted primarily to seize women and com-pensate for a sex ratio deficient in females? Eight women of reproduc-tive ages and four children were seized as captives in the 1960s during raids against the Shiriteri and Catrimani. The stated purpose in both raids was revenge for witchcraft in the form of sickness sent by the offending groups against the Mucajai group. Are there any ethnographic indications that the stated reason was not the real reason?

Nineteen different men were involved in the raiding parties; five married, two betrothed, and twelve single. Two married men took additional wives. Seven of the single men took captive wives and five did not. This does not mean that the man who physically seized the female captive necessarily took her as wife. Accounts of the Catrimani raid show that when the fighting began, all the women remained in the village-house with some Mucajai men. When the Mucajai raiders had finishing chasing and killing all the Catrimani men, they seized the women as a group. There was no individual capture. A man signals his intention to take a captive as wife by challenging the access of other males to her. During the return journey one of the women remained without a claimant. The oldest man of the group, probably to get someone to guard and prevent her from returning to a Catrimani village, asked one of the married men if he wanted the captive as wife. He refused and the old man then asked a single man who also refused. Later the old man again asked the married man and this time he took the captive as an additional wife. This type of interaction suggests the taking of female captives as a secondary aspect of raiding. Female seizure is part of the revenge and provides a spoil for the victor, but it is not the motive for the raid itself. Cocco (1972) also found this in the southwestern area. The formation of the raiding party itself is usually determined by kinship relations to the person being avenged. Perhaps some of the raiders also hoped to obtain a wife, but this would not be the reason for the raid itself. The stated reasons for this raid are traditional ones in the culture. Lizot (1985), while giving importance to contention over women as a source of conflict, clearly states that it is not the only source. The ethnographic evidence (Cocco, Chagnon, Lizot, Smole) is also strong that revenge for witchcraft which may or may not involve women is also an important source.

V. Cultural Impact of the Missionaries

The influence of cultural factors on demographic variables has been examined in the preceding chapters. The missionaries have been mentioned, but their role in either changing or failing to change the traditional Yanomama culture needs to be made explicit. The goal of the missionaries was to found a self-sustaining Yanomama church based on an evangelical interpretation of the Bible. Biblical translation and instruction were seen as leading to baptism as a sign of Christian commitment. This required church attendance, prayer, personal integrity, and care of one's spouse and children. In terms of specific Yanomama cultural practices different from those of the missionaries, commitment meant renunciation of the practice of or participation in shamanistic rituals, of the use of hallucinogenic drugs, and of alcohol, which was introduced later by other Yanomama groups. The missionaries did not make an issue of Yanomama polygyny or polyandry.

In the 28 postcontact years there have been 25 baptisms among the Mucajai Yanomama, 8 in the 1960s, 12 in the early 1970s, and 5 in the late 1970s. Some of the baptized have since died. In the late 1980s the baptized comprised about 5% of the population. This indicates the slight penetration of Yanomama culture by the religious activity of the missionaries. No customs have been terminated. There is only lessened participation in a few by the small minority of baptized. Neel and Weiss (1975) also agree that there has been little change of the traditional culture. The American mission board, which sponsors the effort, has had doubts about continuing it because of the minimal response by the Yanomama.

The rest of the Mucajai Yanomama have remained indifferent to the religious activity of the missionaries or have explicitly rejected it and reaffirmed their commitment to the patterns rejected by the missionaries. Regardless of their reaction, all in the community have continued to frequent the mission for trade and medical purposes. The Yanomama see these as essential activities of the missionaries and they do not regard their rejection of the religious activity as rejection of the missionaries themselves. The missionaries, in turn, have offered their trade and medical services to all the community without distinction.

VI. Demographic Impact of the Missionaries

To complete the account of the population dynamics of the postcontact period, the impact of the missionaries on the demographic factors needs to be made explicit. The question can be phrased thus: Would the Mucajai population have increased by the same amount and in the same way without the missionaries? The question needs to be distinguished—the factual question and the hypothetical question of what might have been without the missionaries. As for the factual question, it is clear that the missionaries have had a significant impact on the demography.

A. In-Migration

As noted in Table 6.1, the missionaries introduced the Mucajai group to four of the six groups from which they received postcontact in-migration. Of the 58 in-migrants, 42 (72.4%) were from these groups. Also, the missionaries, by supplying medical assistance and trade goods to the Mucajai people, contributed to their prestige in the region. This reputation was important in allowing Mucajai men to quickly return to their own village after a brief period of bride service. It was influential for the village to be seen as a place of refuge by families escaping revenge in their own villages. In-migration was a key factor in changing the age–sex distribution, and the missionaries were a key factor in initiating the in-migration. These demographic effects were never a matter of intentional policy by the missionaries.

B. Out-Migration

The presence of the missionaries was a deterrent to out-migration. Disputes are endemic within Yanomama villages. There is a tendency among the larger Yanomama populations to fission and to maintain quarrels through raids. The Mucajai group has grown from two to six villages in the 28 years. Until recently they remained in close interaction and defined themselves as a distinct people. The forces of integration were able to prevail over the forces of dispersion due to the missionaries. The convenient supply of trade goods ar ' the medical attention kept these groups around the mission station. This proximity resulted in social interaction and overcame the tendency to fission into distinct and hostile villages. There have been disputes and fights among the Mucajai villages, but they have never reached a level where they threatened to disband the group and send fissioning groups fleeing into the jungle, perhaps never to see some of their people again. Although the level of conflict in this area is not as intense, Chagnon's data from the southwestern sector shows that this is a latent possibility in Yanomama culture. This absence of fissioning has played an important role in the high rate of increase and was a completely unintended consequence of the missionaries' activity.

C. Mortality

The missionaries have also lowered the level of mortality. There was less preferential female infanticide according to the testimony of the Yanomama. It is not known whether this was a significant decrease or not. The missionaries know of only two cases where their influence prevented female infanticides. Medical assistance has lowered morbidity and consequently mortality by an unknown amount. The mission has also lessened mortality by supplying trade goods. The Mucajai people had an insatiable desire for steel tools and, without the missionaries, would have made many more downstream trips to obtain them. This would have increased the frequency of their contacts with rural Brazilians and consequently with infectious disease and alcoholism. The missionaries also mitigated mortality by acting as a restraining force against raids and the accompanying homicides. When Mucajai men were killed by unknown Yanomama and presumably by Xiriana, their kin spoke openly of retaliatory raids. The missionaries helped to calm the situation so that these raids never materialized. Finally, the presence of the missionaries deterred raids by other Yanomama. None occurred. It is impossible to quantify how much the missionaries lowered the mortality of the Mucajai, but their presence was a significant factor in the low mortality of phase 2 and the moderate mortality of phase 3.

D. Fertility

There is no evidence of any significant missionary influence on the Mucajai reproductive customs. Abortion was seldom discussed by the missionaries. The mitigation of infanticide means that some women had longer birth intervals for the following birth. The effect on the level of fertility appears inconsequential.

VII. Demographic Change without the Missionaries

Would the same demographic results have occurred without the missionaries? In other words, did the missionaries merely accelerate the time frame of demographic change in the traditional Yanomama culture? Such hypothetical questions are difficult to answer, but the following is conjectured. In regard to the isolation from other indigenous groups, it appears that the Mucajai group would have eventually made contacts. On one of the downstream trips before the arrival of the missionaries, they saw Aica groups but did not contact them. Later they probably would have established contact and, through the Aica, would have made contact with the Catrimani. They had entered into contact with the Marashiteri independent of the missionaries. The Marashiteri had their own independent contacts with the Paramiteri who, in turn, had contacts with the Xiriana. Eventually they would probably have introduced the Mucajai people to these groups. Therefore it appears that interaction leading to in-migration would have eventually taken place. But as previously noted, this would probably have been offset by out-migration from fissioning and for marriage. The balance of net migration is impossible to estimate.

There does not appear to be any factor that could have substituted for the missionaries' influence on mortality. But it is difficult to measure this impact and its significance for the overall population dynamics.

In summary, even though this research studies a foraging/horticultural group from the first moment of permanent contact, and even though the missionaries have not effected significant change in the traditional Yanomama culture, there is no claim that all aspects of the study represent the population dynamics of such a group in the precontact period or of early man. The research presents some materials that could contribute to such a discussion, but it would require an extensive and speculative exposition that would distract from the primary task here.

VIII. Sexual Imbalance in the Precontact Population

The discussion of this question was postponed since its analysis required familiarity with the dynamics of the postcontact period. At the time of contact, females comprised 36.4% of the total population of 121. If sexual balance is considered normal (or near balance granting that there are slightly more males at birth with an average sex ratio of approximately 105), then the 36.4% poses a problem.

However, this research has shown that demographic volatility is an essential characteristic of this type of society. This volatility touches all four demographic variables so that it can affect the population structure in many ways. Volatility is highly probable as a factor for the sexual imbalance in a population of this size. In other words, balance is not necessarily normal.

In addition, the precontact history, although fragmented, clearly cites instances of out-migration in which female captives were taken from this group. It is also probable that other women left for marriage. Fissioning occurred, although its sexual composition is unknown. Departing groups may have had more females. While the data are fragmentary, it is possible that out-migration contributed to sexual imbalance.

Female mortality is definitely another factor. The Yanomama testify that there was more preferential female infanticide in the precontact period. Infanticide was mitigated in the postcontact period because of the influence of the missionaries.

Therefore the factors contributing to the sexual imbalance found at the time of contact were: demographic volatility, preferential female infanticide, out-migration in the forms of women taken as captives, probably some for marriage and possibly some because of fissioning. What is the importance or relative weight of each of these factors? To answer this more important question requires a specific type and quality of quantitative data which are unavailable. There is some information and quantitative data, which permit speculation, but they cannot get beyond speculation to probability or certitude.

In populations of 100 to 150 people, it is highly probable that demographic volatility will be an important factor. This is especially true of the sex ratio at birth since only a small percentage of the population gives birth each year. It is clear that out-migration is a factor, but its importance could range from very little to very great.

It is difficult to assign any probability to the impact of female infanticide. Part of this difficulty arises from the testimony of the Yanomama. Their cognitive categories for counting are limited. What is translated in English as "many" means for them "more than two." In the postcontact period preferential female infanticide occurred after 1.8% of all births. The Yanomama testimony means more than this, but gives no indication of how much more because "many" is an ambiguous translation. A male is desired as the first birth of a mother. The fertility histories contain data on the sex of first-order births in the precontact period as shown in Table 8.4. Small-number volatility

Table 8.4
First Births by Sex, Precontact Period

Year	Male	Female	Total
1900s	5	3	8
1910s	4	0	4
1920s	5	1	6
1930s	5	1	6
1940s	3	2	5
1950s	3	3	6
Postcontact	25	28	53

immediately causes a problem of interpretation. If balance is taken as normal, then the deficit of females is concentrated between 1910 and the 1930s. This is also observed in the age–sex distribution at contact (Table 2.2). The 36.4% percent overall female deficit is primarily due to the deficit in ages 20–44, or those born 1914 to 1938. They constitute only 16.3% of this age group. If preferential female infanticide were the overwhelming reason for the deficit, it would probably be spread over all the time periods. Instead the grouping within certain years suggests a factor which would more likely be concentrated in time, such as out-migration.

Table 8.5 examines the number of successive female births since preferential female infanticide would limit these possibilities. Given the small numbers and the weakness of some of the precontact data, these data do not permit an assessment of the importance of preferential female infanticide in the precontact period.

In summary, random volatility, female infanticide, and possibly out-migration in one or several forms are factors contributing to the 36.4% female proportion of the population at the time of contact. There is no evidence that any one factor by itself is largely responsible for the proportion.

Table 8.5
Number of Successive Female Birth (SFB) Groups, Number of Females, and Percentage of Births

No. in successive female births	1900–1939	1940–1958	1959–1986
2	3	4	20
3	1		5
4			2
5			1
x^a	$1(2)^a$	$3(4)$	
No. females in successive female births	11	12	68
No. births	93	65	279
Females in SFB as % of births	16.9%	18.4%	24.4%

^{a}x = groups of female births that overlapped time periods; ( ) represents the number of females in groups born in the period.

IX. Conclusion

This chapter synthesizes the population dynamics of the Mucajai group in the postcontact period. It suggests the outlines of three distinct situations through which foraging/horticultural groups may pass as they come into contact with elements of the national culture in which their territory is located. The small natural increase of the first phase is caused by the immediate impact of high mortality from infectious disease among a group without previous natural immunity. The second phase represents a period of mortality decline. The group acquires some immunity against infectious disease and is helped by a small medical program and by restricted contact with the national society. The third phase represents the beginning of integration into the rural sector of the national society and the transition to peasantry. For some groups this might begin a period of depopulation. Other groups appear to move directly from the first to the third phase without the intermediate one, which may be more typical of an isolated group with missionary presence. The urgent need is more studies with reliable data before comparative analysis and typologies with analytical power begin to emerge.

Nine

The Effect of Changed Demographic
Structures on Cultural Patterns

The previous chapter explained how the sex ratio at birth and patterns of in-migration were mainly responsible for changing the age–sex structure of the Mucajai population in the postcontact period. This chapter examines the feedback from the changed age–sex structure on the cultural patterns of sexual unions and of mother-in-law avoidance.

I. Change of the Sex Ratio

There was a severe shortage of females relative to the number of males in the Mucajai population at the time of contact. They comprised only 36.4% of the total group, and only 22.6% of the female reproductive group, ages 15 to 44. This sexual imbalance evolved to balance during the postcontact period as shown in Fig. 9.1. In 1987 the number of females almost equaled the males in the total population and they comprised a slight majority within the female reproductive ages. This change of the sex composition has been accompanied by changes

103

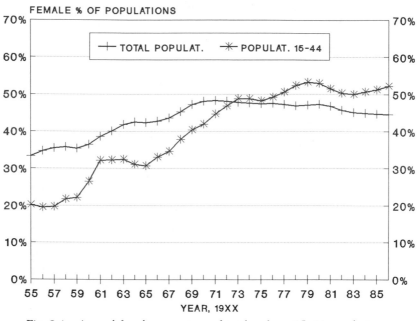

Fig. 9.1 Annual female percentage of total and age 15–44 populations.

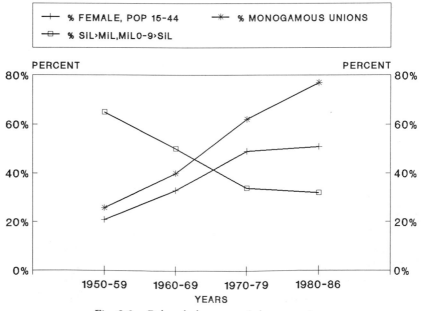

Fig. 9.2 Cultural changes and the sex ratio.

in the cultural patterns shown in Fig. 9.2 With a balanced sex ratio, there has been a sharp swing in the predominant type of sexual union from polyandry to monogamy. The balanced sex ratio has also resulted in a decrease of age differences between married couples. This, in turn, resulted in an increase in the age differences between sons-in-law and mothers-in-law. And this in turn has led to a change in the observance of the mother-in-law avoidance patterns.

I. Change of Types of Sexual Unions

Mate selection was treated briefly in Chapter 4, where the discussion of the reproductive span used the example of a young man seeking a wife. Other patterns and complications were not described because they do not directly affect fertility, the focus of Chapter 4. When a man seeks a wife, a primary consideration is a mate who stands in the cross-cousin classification to him. Age is not an important consideration. Frequently in the first marriage the male will be older than the female simply because there are more younger females who are not married. But the male will frequently have already been a father because of a sharing relationship with the wife of an older man. A few men, usually those of high prestige, will acquire another wife and very rarely a third.

There is immense complexity of types of Yanomama sexual unions. Identification of all the logical possibilities is a difficult task which the Yanomama themselves do not undertake. Given the information in the database and the analytical purpose of this chapter, Table 9.1 develops a sixfold classification of sexual unions to show their structural changes during the postcontact period. Each birth in the database includes an identity code for the mother and fathers, who are distinguished as primary or secondary fathers. Ethnographic information along with the various types of paternities are used as indicators of the types of sexual unions preceding the births. The birth frequencies indicate the prevalence and endurance of the various types of sexual unions from 1950 to 1987.

There was one group marriage involving four people which resulted in births during the 1950s and 1960s. Births with a single primary father married to only one female at that time are monogamous unions. A birth with a single primary father who at the same time was

Table 9.1
Number and Percentage of Births by Type of Sexual Union at Time of Birth

Years	Total	Group marriage	Monogamy	Polygyny	Residential polyandry	Visiting polyandry +	No marriage
Number of births							
1950s	27	4	7	3	9	4	0
1960s	57	2	23	7	6	17	2
1970s	113	0	70	12	5	25	1
1980s	107	0	82	7	4	6	8
Total	304	6	182	29	24	52	11
Percentage of births							
1950s	100%	15%	26%	11%	33%	15%	0%
1960s	100	4	40	12	11	30	4
1970s	100	0	62	11	4	22	1
1980s	100	0	77	7	4	6	7
Total	100%	2%	60%	10%	8%	17%	4%
d, 1950s–1980s		−15%	+51%	−4%	−29%	−9%	+7%

married to one or more women is a polygynous union. Examples of this type were several important shamans who had two or three wives and older men who took young wives with their first wives remaining.

A husband may share his wife or wives with other men. The sharing male may be a younger household brother, another type of kin, or a nonkin. The sharing male has his meals prepared by the shared female. In this chapter this situation will be called residential polyandry. Table 9.2 shows its frequency. The sharing male may also be a

Table 9.2
Structure of Polyandry: Fraternal and Nonfraternal; Extent of Wife Sharing[a]

Years	Residential polyandry			Visiting polyandry +		
	n	B-NB	S-P	n	B-NB	S-P
1950s	9	5-4	6-3	4	0-4	2-2
1960s	6	0-6	5-1	17	6-11	9-8
1970s	5	1-4	5-0	25	7-18	22-3
1980s	4	0-4	4-0	6	3-3	5-1
Total	24	6-18	20-4	52	16-36	38-14

[a]Abbreviations: B, cases where at least one secondary husband is a brother to the primary husband; NB, cases where no brothers of primary husband among secondary husbands; S, cases of a single sharing male in the polyandrous relation; P, cases of two or more sharing males in the polyandrous relation.

member of another household. These situations will be called visiting polyandry. Some instances involve a combination of both. (Polyandry is a disputed term in anthropology and the usage here is mere convenience without entering into these disputes.) The importance of polyandry among the Mucajai group appears to have increased during the period of isolation. Migliazza (1964) does not mention it in his discussion of marriage forms among the Xiriana Ninam who fissioned from the Mucajai group before the period of isolation began. The number of recognized fathers for a single child in these polyandrous relations can vary from two to a case of eight.

The visiting polyandry category overlaps with the last category of no marriage. No marriage includes cases of separated and widowed women who gave birth and some known cases of sexual union without consent of the primary husband but in which the paternity is recognized. Some of the cases listed under visiting polyandry are probably cases of no marriage. This is symbolized by the + sign in the table. These are cases where it is not certain that consent existed. Sometimes a relationship will begin as clandestine and afterward be accepted as a recognized polyandrous relation. At times the difference between the two types can be very slight. Ethnographic knowledge was insufficient to distinguish all the cases with certitude.

Table 9.2 indicates that nonfraternal polyandry ("B" in table) was more prevalent than fraternal polyandry in both residential and nonresidential forms. Given the patrilineal structure of the Yanomama, this is somewhat unexpected. While the reason is not certain, it appears that the shortage of women was not uniformly spread in all lineages. Some were not as deficient, hence there was less pressure for polyandry. Others had severe shortages and thus sought sharing wives from other lineages. This situation would by definition be nonfraternal polyandry.

In Table 9.1 the most significant change over the postcontact period is the increase of births from monogamous unions. They rose from 26% during the 1950s to 77% in the 1980s. This is correlated with the increase in the female proportion of the reproductive population from 22.6% at the time of contact to 53.2% in 1987 (Fig. 9.1, Table 8.2). As the sexual imbalance was reduced, monogamous sexual unions increased rapidly. This suggests that at contact the dominance (over 70% of polyandrous and group marriages was influenced by the shortage of reproductive females. Lizot (1985) mentions three polyandrous cases in a Yanomamo village and attributes it to a deficiency of kinship eligible females. He gives no indication of how extensive it was. He also details the inferior status of secondary husbands and the reasons males would want to change to monogamy. In the 1980s only 10% of the births were from wife-sharing unions. Not only did the incidence of partner sharing drop, but Table 9.2 shows that the number of sharing partners decreased in unions where sharing was continued. Births from unions with more than one sharing partner ("P" in table) declined from 38% of the births in the 1950s to 11% in the 1980s. In summary, the increase in the female percentage of the population from imbalance to balance was accompanied by an increase in monogamy and a decrease in polyandry (as defined here) and, where polyandry was retained, a decrease in the number of sharing males.

III. Mother-in-Law Avoidance

The Yanomama have culturally prescribed patterns of mother-in-law avoidance. Throughout his marriage, the primary husband does not speak to his mother-in-law. No words are exchanged when offering gifts or performing services for the bride price. If the two should meet by chance on the trail, there is some embarrassment. The mother-in-law lowers her head and steps off the trail into the forest to let the son-in-law pass. This pattern of cultural behavior is prescribed for all mother-in-law–son-in-law relationships in all circumstances. It is one reason why males try to shorten the period of bride service.

The presence of such strong avoidance patterns may appear somewhat puzzling to individuals from youth-oriented cultures as exemplified in many parts of the industrialized world. The usual generational age differences between mothers-in-law and sons-in-law in developed societies, the availability of women of similar age, living arrangements, and moral precepts all mitigate sexual encounters between these kin. In Yanomamo society these barriers are not as strong. During the several years of bride service, the son-in-law is living within the same dwelling and at times the same family group as his mother-in-law, in physically very close quarters. The age difference between these two in-laws is an open question in Yanomama society. Table 9.3 shows the age differences between couples (mothers and primary

Table 9.3

Years Difference in Age at Time of Births between Males and Females in Monogamous, Polygynous, and Polyandrous Unions

Age difference (years)	Number of births					Percentage				
	1950	1960	1970	1980	Total	1950	1960	1970	1980	Total
M > F 40+	1	1	3	1	6	4.3	1.9	2.7	1.0	2.1
30	2	5	5	1	13	8.7	9.4	4.5	1.0	4.5
20	7	10	17	16	50	30.4	18.9	15.2	16.2	17.4
10	0	12	38	29	79	0.0	22.6	33.9	29.3	27.5
0	12	18	42	42	114	52.2	34.0	37.5	42.4	39.7
F > M 0	0	4	7	7	18	0.0	7.5	6.3	7.0	6.3
10	0	3	0	3	6	0.0	5.7	0.0	3.0	2.1
20+	1	0	0	0	1	4.3	0.0	0.0	0.0	.3
Total	23	53	112	99	287	100	100	100	100	100
M > F 20+						43.4	30.2	22.4	18.2	24.0

fathers) for each birth in the database. The range covered by the scale is about 75 years. There are some cases where the father is over 45 years older than the mother and where the mother is over 25 years older than the husband. The cases of a much older male usually involve captive girls or men marrying young women after the previous wife has passed menopause. Cocco (1972) has also noted that there can be large age disparity between spouses among the southwestern Yanomamo. Lizot (1985) cites a case where the difference was 35 years.

This disparity between the ages of married couples means that the mother-in-law can be younger than or about the same age as the son-in-law. Table 9.3 shows that in 24% of unions, the primary husband is 20 or more years older than the wife. In these instances, his mother-in-law may be younger or of a similar age. The analysis needs to establish a rule of thumb to determine a cutoff point where the mother-in-law may be considered of a similar age as the son-in-law. Cases where the mother-in-law is up to 10 years older than the son-in-law can be used. Table 9.4 indicates that 17% of the sons-in-law were older than their mother-in-law. In 22% of the cases the mother-in-law is less than 10 years older than the son-in-law. Consequently, in about 39% of the marital situations but 65% in the 1950s there is the potential of heightened sexual competition because of this age structure. The mother-in-law–son-in-law relationship is incestuous by kin definition

Table 9.4

Years Difference in Age at Time of Births between Sons-in-Law and Mothers-in-Law

Age difference (years)	Number of births					Percentage				
	1950	1960	1970	1980	Total	1950	1960	1970	1980	Total
MiL > SiL[a] 40+	1	0	2	5	8	5.0	0.0	3.1	6.8	4.1
30	0	1	5	12	18	0.0	2.6	7.7	16.4	9.2
20	3	12	17	17	49	15.0	31.6	26.2	23.3	25.0
10	3	6	19	16	44	15.0	15.8	29.2	21.9	22.4
0	12	12	8	11	43	60.0	31.6	12.3	15.1	21.9
SiL > MiL 0	1	5	8	10	24	5.0	13.2	12.3	14.0	12.2
10	0	2	6	2	10	0.0	5.3	9.2	2.7	5.1
20+	0	0	0	0	0	0.0	0.0	0.0	0.0	0.0
Total	20	38	65	73	196	100	100	100	100	100
% of MiLs younger or less than 10 years older than SiL						65.0	50.1	33.8	31.8	39.2

[a]Abbreviations: MiL, mother-in-law; SiL, son-in-law.

if they become sexual partners. Because of the age structure, Yano-mama culture provides extra protection in the form of the strong avoidance patterns.

The Yanomamo myth of the incestuous son-in-law clearly confirms these demographic reasons for the mother-in-law avoidance patterns. Three versions of this myth have been collected in different Yano-mamo villages by Lizot (1975) and Cocco (1972). The myth was elic-ited by Cocco from a Yanomamo leader in reply to a direct question about the reason for the patterns of avoidance.

The following version is translated from Lizot's (1975) Spanish ren-dering of the version from Karohitheri. It is the most detailed and graphic of the three.

A village had been invited to a feast in another village. On the jour-ney, the group made camp for the night at a place still some distance from the village where the feast was to be held. The next morning when the group arose, a short man by the name of Bat reclined in his ham-mock with his arm folded behind his head.

Someone said: "Let's get going. Take down the hammocks. We must paint and adorn ourselves for the feast."

They took out the balls of ochre used to paint themselves along with the feathers and other adornments taken from birds. Bat did not move. He remained in his hammock and said: "I will join you later."

The others left except Bat and his family. Bat called his wife who had thick pubic hair [as Lizot notes, a Yanomamo expression for a beautiful woman] and said: "Don't go to the feast, but remain here alone. They have invited me. They want to trick me when I get there. Tell your mother to pack her hammock and go with me. If they kill me at the feast, she can bring back my head."

The wife went over to her mother.

"Mother, he demands that you go with him."

The mother was very happy to hear that her son-in-law wanted her to go with him. Quickly she put her hammock in a basket and was ready. [The Cocco version of the myth emphasizes the physical beauty of the mother-in-law.]

Bat said to his wife: "Give my hammock to your mother so she can carry it."

His mother-in-law left. He waited a few minutes and also left. He caught up with his mother-in-law. The sun was going down on the horizon.

He said: "Mother-in-law, let us stay here for the night. We can make a shelter here in the forest. We can catch up with the rest of the group in the morning."

They were close to the village where the feast was to be held. They could hear the men snapping the strings of their bows and yelling while they circled around the opening in the middle of shabono. Bat cut poles for the shelter, put them in place, tied them together and went to look for leaves for the roof. Meanwhile the mother-in-law cut the small strips which were placed on the roof to support the leaves. She could hear shouting from the village as they prepared for the feast.

The mother-in-law said: "Let's forget this shelter and go to the village. It is very close. You can hear them cutting trees for the troughs to cook the food."

Bat said: "It is only the pecking of a peacock."

The mother-in-law said: "Can't you hear them dancing?"

Bat replied: "No, those are the noises of crested oropendola birds who are excited about something."

Night was approaching. When the darkness was complete, Bat broke off a branch with an ant's nest on it and put it near the shelter. He broke open the nest. The ants came out and climbed up the poles of the shelter.

After he reclined in his hammock, Bat yelled: "There are ants here biting me."

The mother-in-law, pretending to observe the mother-in-law avoidance of the son-in-law, turned her back and said nothing.

Bat again yelled: "I can't sleep because of the ants! Mother-in-law!"

"What is it?" she replied.

"There are ants here."

"Then sleep on the other side of the shelter," she replied.

The ants had not yet reached that side, but Bat wanted to lie with his mother-in-law in her hammock. He continued his efforts. Fixing his hammock on the other side of the shelter, he put the nest of ants by his side. Immediately he cried: "They are here too."

The mother-in-law said: "There are none here. Hang your hammock over mine."

Bat was glad to move a little closer to his mother-in-law. He took his hammock down and hung it over his mother-in-law's hammock. He carefully placed the ants' nest under the roof exactly above his hammock. He parted the leaves so that the ants fell on him.

"Mother-in-law, they are here too and they are biting fiercely."

She replied: "Lay down beside me in my hammock, but lay so your feet are next to my face."

He put the nest over his head and continued to complain. He finally succeeded in laying face to face with his mother-in-law. That is what he wanted. He stopped talking about the ants tormenting him. The mother-in-law opened her thighs and gave herself to him. He did not withdraw after ejaculating, his foreskin was partially folded over itself leaving exposed a part of the gland. The penis remained in the vagina like a fish hook caught in the mouth of a fish.

Morning came. He withdrew his penis. They took down their hammocks and put them in the basket. He painted himself with red dye and with his finger tips, marked his forehead with wavy bands. They went to the village where there was loud talking. When they were at the entrance of the village, he was transformed into an animal, a bat which fluttered about and then flew away to a hole in a tree. The mother-in-law changed into a great anteater and fled to a hill where she rolled around on the ground thrashing her thick tail.

The transformation of humans into animals is a frequent theme in Indian mythology. It often signifies severe punishment for committing great evil as defined by cultural standards. The Cocco version is more explicit on this point. The myth clearly shows the Yanomama fear of this type of incest and its expression in the patterns of mother-in-law avoidance. It could create explosive tensions within the kin group and therefore must be controlled, especially in a culture that is completely structured by kinship.

Among the Mucajai people, the change in the sex ratio from imbalance to balance has affected the observance of the avoidance patterns. Tables 9.3 and 9.4 show that, with the change of the sex ratio, the age difference between marriage partners has declined. Consequently the age difference between sons-in-law and mothers-in-law has increased. As a result the observance of the avoidance patterns was much weaker in the mid-1980s than at the time of contact. Ethnographic information indicates that mothers-in-law and sons-in-law do not take the avoidance pattern as seriously and interact in situations where they previously did not. This is also due to the increased contact with outsiders including the missionaries. But within the culture, the main reason is that the need for the avoidance pattern has been mitigated by the changing age structure of marriage. Table 9.3 shows that there has been a decrease in the age difference between primary husband and wife. Forty three percent of these unions had at least a 20-year age difference in the 1950s and this had diminished to 18% in the 1980s. As a result, Table 9.4 shows that the percentage of unions where the son-in-law is older than the mother-in-law or the mother-in-law was less than 10 years older than the son-in-law declined from 65% in the 1950s to 32% in the 1980s. Most of this decline is in the group where the mother-in-law is less than 10 years older than the son-in-law. Over one-half of all the cases were in this category in the 1950s. In the 1960s this had fallen to 31% of the cases. In the next two phases, the shift was in the direction of the mother-in-law being more than 10 years older than the son-in-law. Chagnon (1977) cites an example where a village leader no longer bothered to avoid his mother-in-law because she was an old woman. The ethnographic information clearly confirms the importance of the relative ages for the mother-in-law avoidance patterns.

IV. Resources and Population Increase

A question may arise about the ability of the Mucajai people to provide for the large increase of their population over the postcontact period. The physical resources of the region supplied all the subsistence needs of the increased population without difficulty. Horticulture, hunting, gathering, and fishing provided an ample food supply. One reason for village fissioning was to begin new gardens when the old ones declined in yield, but there was no problem with availability of land. Some reduction in the availability of game was noticed and was also a cause of fissioning. There has never been a serious problem of resources and the ability of the Mucajai group to provide for their increased population.

V. Conclusion

This completes the analysis of demographic structure and culture. The previous chapter has shown how fertility with a balanced sex ratio at birth and free or captive female in-migration for marriage changed the age–sex distribution of the Mucajai group, especially by reducing the imbalanced sex ratio of the reproductive population. This chapter has shown how a changed age–sex structure has, in turn, changed the intensity of two cultural patterns. There was an increase in monogamous marriages and a corresponding decrease in polyandrous marriages. Where wife-sharing was retained, there was a diminution of the number of males in the sharing networks. The change in the

Table 9.5
Schematic of Principal Demographic and Cultural Changes

Cultural and demographic variables	In-migration			Change in cultural and demographic variables		
	Reason	n	Total			
Disease as witchcraft	Revenge raids	2 M 9 F 11				
Imbalanced sex ratio and prestige of Mucajai group	Marriage	11 M 17 F 58	24 M 34 F 58 total	More balanced sex ratio	Increase in monogamy	
			41% M 59% F (68% F of Reproductive ages)		Decrease in age differential at marriage	Decreased mother-in law avoidance
Fear of revenge	Refuge	8 M 5 F 13		Increase in group fertility	Lower median age	Lower mortality (phase 2)
Other		3 M 3 F 6				

age–sex distribution also diminished the age difference between marital partners. This, in turn, increased the age differences between mothers-in-law and sons-in-law, thereby reducing potential sexual conflict within family groups. As a result the avoidance patterns between mothers-in-laws and sons-in-laws have diminished. Table 9.5 gives a synoptic view of these changes. In brief, the synthetic section has shown how culture affects the demographic structure of a population (Chapter 8), and how this, in turn, affects the intensity of some cultural patterns (Chapter 9).

PART FOUR

Conclusion

Ten

Yanomama Population Dynamics

The preceding chapters have investigated the population dynamics of a Ninam Yanomama group living on the middle Mucajai River in Brazil. In this final chapter the question is raised about the implications of this study for other Yanomama groups, and more generally about the population dynamics and demography of foraging/horticultural groups. How typical are the Mucajai Ninam of other Yanomama groups, especially the Yanomamo and the Yanomam? The Sanema are omitted because they are intermingled with the Maquiritare (Yekwana), which has led to linguistic and cultural changes. To examine this problem, we shall first look at the ethnographic question. Are the cultural patterns surrounding the demographic variables similar in the south central and southwestern Yanomama regions? Then the demographic question will be asked: Are the quantitative levels of these patterns similar? What light does this study throw on previous information about the demography of these groups?

I. Cultural Patterns

A. Fertility

The cultural patterns surrounding fertility were described in Chapter 4. The patterns of betrothal, menstruation rite, cohabitation, and birth appear to be universal in the Yanomama region. Much the same description is given by Cocco (1972), Lizot (1985), and Chagnon (1983) for the Yanomamo or southwestern region. The pattern of lactation as well as the use of abortion and infanticide appear to be common to all areas. Cocco (1972) gives the same list of reasons for the practice of abortion and infanticide as found in Table 7.3 of this study. The only difference is marital discord as a separate reason, but this is probably more of an editorial than a real difference. Chagnon (1977) also found the maintenance of spacing for the sake of the nursling an important reason, as well as preferential female infanticide. Lizot (1985) and Smole (1976) remark that infants sleep in the hammock with their mothers during the night. This means that the contraceptive effect of lactation is possible throughout the full 24-hour period. Chagnon (1977) also found in the southwestern area a cultural norm of postpartum abstinence from sexual relations during the lactation period of an infant, but it is frequently not followed for the entire period.

The high incidence of polyandry in the early postcontact period may be unique to the Mucajai group, but there is no indication that it has a differential effect on fertility. It probably developed during the generation of isolation as a way of compensating for the unbalanced sex ratio. Cocco (1972) and Lizot (1985) found some polyandry in the southeastern region. In situations of a shortage of females for marriage, Lizot (1985), Cocco (1972), and Chagnon (1977) found some temporary homosexuality. Lizot says it is frequently between brothers-in-law whose wives have not yet reached maturity. Cocco (1972) notes restricted polygyny among the southwestern Yanomamo.

B. Migration

In-migration and out-migration because of marriage, fissioning, seeking refuge from conflict in another village, or capture in a raid are frequently cited in the writings of Cocco, Valero, Chagnon, and Smole. These patterns appear to be universal throughout the Yanomama region. (Valero is a Brazilian woman who was kidnapped from her family's farm by a Yanomamo group when she was 13 years of age. For 24 years, 1932 to 1956, she lived among the Yanomamo, married, had children, and became, in many respects, a Yanomamo. The cited references are to her autobiography or to information Cocco elicited from her when she settled at the mission of Santa Maria after she returned from the Yanomamo. Lizot (1984) has cautioned against accepting all her information at face value.)

C. Mortality

The causes of death in Table 7.1 are similar to Chagnon's (1974) more complete listing for the southwestern area, although there are differences in frequency. Chagnon does not discriminate precontact and postcontact situations and this accounts for some of the difference. Infectious disease transmitted from the outside world is common to all the areas in the postcontact situation. The comparative good health of the Yanomama in precontact or semi-isolated situations has been noticed by Smole (1976), Lizot (1984), and Steinvorth Goetz (1969), a physician with experience in southwestern and south central areas. In the Mucajai data there are no maternal deaths in the 28 years. Cocco (1972) found only one maternal death in his 15 years experience in the southwestern area, which may be the same single case listed by Chagnon (1974). These data reject any assumption of universal high maternal mortality among foraging/horticultural groups.

Protection of the nursling as an important reason for abortion was also found by Cocco (1972). Valero (Cocco 1972) found that among some of the Yanomamo groups with whom she lived, spacing due to the demands of nursing was maintained neither by induced abortion nor infanticide, but by not sufficiently feeding infants so that they died of malnutrition. Although the method is different, this confirms that the primary reason for lengthy spacing is protection of the nursling. Cocco (1972) and Chagnon (1977) found the same reasons for infanticide among the southwestern Yanomamo as among the Ninam.

II. Demographic Levels of the Patterns

A. Methodological Problems of the Studies

While the foregoing analysis shows the cultural patterns entering into the four demographic variables are much the same in the three

Yanomama regions, a further question is whether these cultural (and biological) patterns yield similar demographic frequencies or levels in the different regions. Table 10.1 presents a summary of Yanomama demographic indices either culled or calculated from the extant research. The data are grouped by regions. The Mucajai research represents the southeastern region. Most of the previous research is from the southwestern region, where the quantitative material is heavily dependent on Chagnon's field work although there are some independent data from Lizot. The remaining information is from Smole's collection of demographic data from missionaries in the Parima Highlands. The methodological problems of each of these studies will be discussed and then a comparative analysis made of their results to see what they indicate about the quantitative levels of the demographic variables among the Yanomama.

B. Chagnon

The authors of this investigation, as all students of the Yanomama, are indebted to Chagnon for his research data and teaching materials. From the viewpoint of this investigation, however, it should be noted that Chagnon has never conducted a focused, demographic study in his field research. Most of his demographic data have been generated from census and genealogical materials which were collected for other research objectives. Chagnon uses the word "demographic," but it frequently has the broad meaning of quantified variables of any type rather than the technical demographic sense. As seen in the first column of Table 10.1, Chagnon has used few demographic indices in his published work.

From a demographic perspective, the basic problem has been Chagnon's lack of reliable data on infants and children. For the most part he attempted survey work—13 villages over 11 years. During periodic visits, it was impossible to reconstruct fully all the demographic events (births, infant and child deaths) since the last visit because of problems previously discussed (Chagnon, 1974; Chagnon et al., 1979). A second unsolved problem was age estimation. It was based exclusively on physical appearance, which is never satisfactory (Neel and Chagnon, 1968; Chagnon, 1974). As a result of these limitations of Chagnon's database, there was no satisfactory analysis of fertility and mortality (Chagnon, 1988).

C. Lizot

Lizot followed an opposite strategy by concentrating most of his efforts in a single village of 50 people for 3.5 years. But Lizot also had different research objectives and did not intend to do a demographic study. He has never published a conventional demographic index drawn from his data. Employing his published materials, all the demographic indices in the Lizot column of Table 10.1 were first calculated for construction of the table itself. While Lizot has data on infants and children, the small village and the short time span diminish their value for analytical purposes. Although the problem is not mentioned, it appears that age estimation was also based exclusively on physical appearance. Lizot's data are also included as one of the 13 villages in Chagnon's database.

D. Simulation and Stable Population Models

Because of the limitations of the Chagnon–Lizot database for purposes of demographic analysis, there have been several compensatory attempts using demographic models and simulations: MacCluer *et al.* (1971), Neel and Weiss (1975), and Melancon (1982). The validity of these methods needs examination and will be discussed shortly in the section on the mortality indices.

E. Smole

Smole's research in the Central Highlands suffers from many of the same problems as Lizot's work. The demographic materials were incidental to other research purposes. It is limited to a 2-year time span and no age data are presented apart from very general classifications of little value for demographic analysis.

F. Early–Peters

The Mucajai database employed in this research overcomes a number of the previous limitations. It has a time series of 28 years. Since the postcontact averages group together diverse population dynamics, the time span has been subdivided into the three phases. There are excellent data on births and child mortality. The age data are satisfactory for analytical purposes. The results are presented in the last columns of Table 10.1. They raise questions about some previous findings of the Yanomama demographic literature.

Table 10.1
Survey of Yanomamo Fertility and Mortality Indices

Index	Southwestern					Central	Total	Southeastern		
	1	2	3	4	5	6		7 (Phase)		
								1	2	3
Type of study[b]	F	F	S	S	S	F	F	F	F	F
Years, 19XX	64–74	69–72	66&68	66–71	70–74	68–70	58–86	59–69	70–79	80–86
No. of years	11	3.5	—	—	—	2	28	11	10	7
No. of villages	13	1	4	29	13	1	2–6	2	3	6
No. of Yanomamo	1336	47	451	2600	1326	210	458	—	—	—
Fertility										
Crude Birth	—	62.8	—	57.5	62.4	57.0	49.9	40.0	54.1	50.6
Total Fert.	3.8	—	4.8	[8.2]	7.8	—	7.9	8.7	7.5	7.5
Mortality										
Crude Death	—	62.8	—	48.8	53.0	16.0	23.4	36.3	12.3	26.0
Infant	—	444	300	349	367	—	133	131	78	209
Infant, male	—	—	250	267	383	—	118	—	—	—
Infant, female	—	—	350	430	351	—	167	—	—	—
Infanticide	—	—	150	175	—	—	61	50	53	76
% of Infant[c]	—	—	50	50.1	—	—	43.6	37.5	66.6	36.3

124

e_0 yrs.			20.7	21.7		38.9	32.8	55.1	39.1
q 0	—	—	349	367	—	140	—	—	—
1	—	—	139	226	—	92	—	—	—
5	—	—	88	60	—	35	—	—	—
10	—	—	102	50	—	49	—	—	—
20	—	—	145	86	—	190	—	—	—
30	—	—	152	114	—	114	—	—	—
40	—	—	160	156	—	139	—	—	—
50	—	—	183	224	—	323	—	—	—
60	—	—	306	359	—	485	—	—	—
70	—	—	521	258	—	—	—	—	—
% Female									
Population	45.8	50.0	45.8	—	51.0	45.2	41.8	52.4	54.5
Births	43.5	54.5	41.7	46.9	50.0	48.4	56.6	48.2	43.8

[a]References: (1) Neel and Chagnon (1968); Chagnon et al., (1979); (2) Lizot (1971); (3) MacCluer et al. (1971); (4) Neel and Weiss (1975); (5) Melancon (1982); (6) Smole (1976); (7) Early and Peters, this volume.

[b]Abbreviations: F. field study; S simulation or projection by models.

[c]% of Infant, percentage of the infant death rate due to infanticide.

III. Fertility

All crude birth rates in Table 10.1 indicate that the Yanomama are a high-fertility population compared with the fertility levels of industrial countries. Most of the total fertility rates indicate about 8 as the average number of live births to a Yanomama female. Chagnon's early finding of a relatively low 3.8 level appears to have been due to deficient data. It is not clear if he included infanticides and other infant deaths in his fertility figures. He may have been thinking of effective fertility, but this is a poorly defined concept and useless for most demographic analysis (Early, 1985). This low fertility rate for Yanomamo women influenced much of the earlier discussion of Yanomamo population dynamics. Chagnon (1968) compared the spacing of the Yanomamo fertility pattern to that of industrialized populations. The rate reported by MacCluer et al. (1971) was heavily influenced by the Chagnon rate.

Neel and Weiss (1975) established an average level of individual fertility. They used physical examinations of 277 Yanomama women and urine specimens from 301 to estimate pregnancy rates. Ages were estimated from physical appearance. A total pregnancy rate was calculated from the age-specific rates. The authors call it a total fertility rate but, as they mention, it is a pregnancy rate. (In the table, unconventional rates are enclosed in brackets to indicate that these figures cannot be directly compared with others.) Since this rate does not consider fetal deaths, it exaggerates the total fertility level by an unknown amount. However it appears to be a good estimate if compared with the Mucajai rates, which are only slightly lower, and most of the difference could be fetal mortality. The two studies establish a relatively high individual fertility rate for the Yanomama. Chagnon et al. (1979) determined the average spacing period between births as 3.4 years. If this is based on good data (which need not be complete), it confirms the Mucajai spacing average of 3.2 years. It indicates that if Chagnon had been able to get complete fertility data, he would have derived a total fertility rate close to that indicated by the Neel-Weiss and Mucajai studies.

There is a question about the level of group fertility. The data from the Mucajai area indicate a crude rate of 50. The crude birth rates of around 60 for the southwestern and central area indicate a higher level. However, the studies of Lizot and Smole were for very short periods of time and may have caught these villages at the highest level of volatility for fertility rates. Figure 4.2 shows that some short spans of Mucajai data yield similar averages. It indicates the necessity of longer time series to analyze the structure. There is also the possibility that the extremely high group fertility level is partially due to the age–sex structure of these populations, for which reliable age data were unavailable. The higher group levels of fertility from the modeling studies are due to assumptions made about mortality. A very high level of fertility was required to overcome high infant and child mortality to make the model work. Questions will be asked about these levels of mortality.

IV. Migration

Neither in-migration nor out-migration received demographic treatment in any previous studies. One reason is because the unit of analysis is never formally discussed. Chagnon pooled his data from 11 villages and all or some of the data were employed by the simulation and models. In much of his work it appears that the unit of analysis was a population bloc consisting of two subblocs, the Shamatari and Namoweiteri villages. Perhaps migration in and out of these subblocs was minimal so that migration could be ignored in spite of considerable migration within the subblocs. On the other hand, the data from Lizot and Smole each represent a single village. The discussions in the literature of village fissioning, marriage, and taking captives suggest that migration cannot be ignored where the unit of analysis is a single village. The unit of analysis of this study has been a population bloc which grew from two to six villages in the time covered by the database. Migration into and out of this population was examined in Chapter 6, and Chapter 8 indicated its importance in the population dynamics.

V. Mortality

The crude rates from Lizot's study are about the same as the high rates in the annual variation of Mucajai crude death rates (Fig. 7.1). They are from a village which had suffered an epidemic of infectious disease due to outside contact. Smole's rates are about the same as the low rates for the Macajai. They are from relatively isolated villages closely resembling phase 2 of this study.

The remaining estimates of mortality, including all age schedules, are dependent on the use of simulation and population models. The simulation by MacCluer *et al.* (1971) was based on early interpretations of Chagnon's data including high female infanticide and relatively low fertility. The weakness of the input data, as the authors mention, together with these assumptions yielded questionable results.

The studies of Neel and Weiss (1975) and Melancon (1982) employed models which yield a picture of extremely high mortality for the Yanomama, with a life expectancy at birth of about 21 years and a crude death rate of 60. While there may be regional variations of Yanomama mortality rates, and warfare is known to be more intense in the southwestern than in the southeastern region, these levels of mortality are extremely high for any human population. This raises some questions about the use of the models to determine Yanomama mortality levels. There are two basic problems with these studies: (1) use of model life tables drawn from populations distinct in mortality structure from the Yanomama, and (2) use of the assumptions of stationarity or stability for Yanomama populations.

A. Model Life Tables

Neel and and Weiss used a set of model tables developed earlier by Weiss (1973). Figure 10.1 shows the age schedule of mortality for each sex of the models used to estimate the Yanomama probabilities of dying. The model where 1(15) = 45 was used for females and where 1(15) = 50 for males. These have been averaged together in Fig. 10.3 to simplify the presentation. Melancon employed the Coale and Demeny (1966) models. Figure 10.2 shows the age patterns of mortality embodied in Coale–Demeny west models for various levels of mortality. The two sex models again are averaged together to simplify presentation. The age pattern of mortality, as expressed by the shape of the curves, is relatively the same regardless of the overall level of mortality. Melancon found that the best fit for his data from 20 to 60 years was the west model with the highest mortality level, a life expectancy of 20 years. Its configuration for the early years was then imposed on the Yanomamo data.

The common characteristics of both models are very high infant

(0–1 year) and early childhood (1–4 years) death rates compared with the rate at age five. When applied to the Yanomamo, this configuration was adjusted by Neel and Weiss for female infanticide so that the disparity was made even greater (Fig. 10.3). If the curves used by the two models are compared with the curve for the Mucajai postcontact period (Fig. 10.3), important differences emerge. In the Mucajai study the levels of infant and early childhood mortality are significantly lower relative to age five than expected by the models. In terms of the graph, the downstroke of the first part of the U-shaped mortality curve is not nearly as pronounced as it is in the model curves. Primarily because of this difference, the models have imposed on Yanomamo demography extremely high crude death rates and extremely low life expectancies at birth.

Why is infant and early childhood mortality so high relative to age five in the models? It is due to the input data and/or assumptions on which the models are based. The Weiss (1973) collection contains a number of populations which are not of the same type as the Yanomama. But more importantly, data for infants and early childhood were highly deficient in this collection. To compensate for this, Weiss (1973) made a number of assumptions that yielded the very high mortality levels. There is no evidence to support the reasonableness of the assumptions. Melancon employed the model tables of Coale and Demeny (1966). The input data for these models were derived by regression analysis from 326 life tables of national populations, i.e., large-scale societies. Sixty-four percent were from Europe and 93% represented populations after 1870. Coale and Demeny (1966) found it necessary to use four different regional patterns of mortality just to summarize these societies and they made no claim that these four were universal. "We must concede that this use of the four families is far from satisfactory, because there is no strong reason for supposing that the age patterns of mortality exhibited in these four families cover anything like the full range of variability in age patterns in populations under different circumstances" (Coale and Demeny, 1966). Anthropological sensitivity would strongly suspect applying patterns from these cultural groups at this stage in their history to Yanomama populations. None of the populations used for the input data had a life expectancy below 35 years. The age pattern for the models with the highest mortality levels were mathematically extrapolated from the lower mortality models.

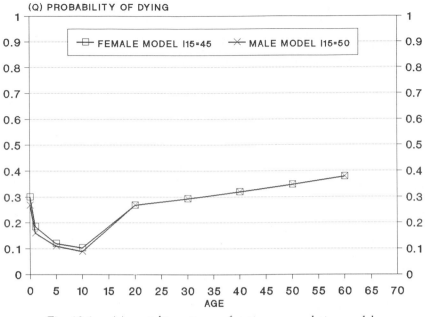

Fig. 10.1 $q(x)$ mortality patterns of stationary population models.

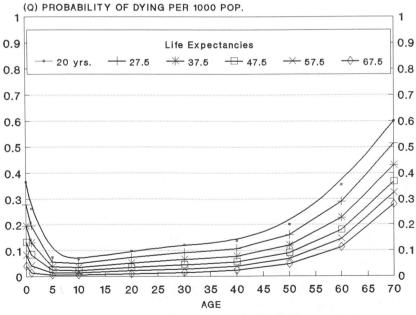

Fig. 10.2 $q(x)$ mortality patterns of Cole–Demeny models.

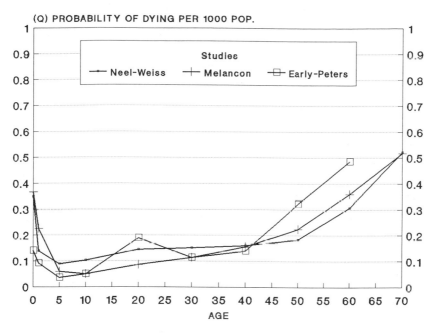

Fig. 10.3 $q(x)$ mortality patterns of Yanomama studies.

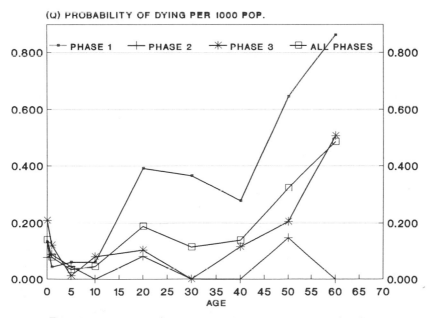

Fig. 10.4 $q(x)$ mortality patterns of Mucajai Yanomama by phases.

B. Stationarity or Stability

The models do not pretend to substitute for incorrect or missing data in any specific time period. The models yield long-run averages. "One is interested in the basic underlying patterns rather than the specific events of a few years" (Neel and Weiss, 1975). ". . . process . . . is a method for estimating the average 'experience' of the population over a prolonged period of time" (Melancon 1982). The long-run averages are seen as analytically useful because both models assume that there is long-run stability in these societies, with Neel–Weiss assuming the most restrictive case of stability, the stationary population.

There are two difficulties with this approach. The Mucajai study has shown that volatility at the village level is an essential characteristic of all demographic variables in Yanomama populations. This means that variations from the averages are so great that the long-run averages themselves become disembodied platonic essences which tell little about any individual village or small group of them. If a larger unit of analysis is used, use of such averages may be helpful for other purposes, but the population dynamics of societies such as the Yanomama cannot be analyzed by considering only the higher levels of aggregation.

Another difficulty is the assumption that Yanomamo populations are a type of stable population, either stationary or quasi-stable. Ethnographic studies have clearly shown that village fissioning involving out-migration, mortality from violence, and in-migration both by captives taken in raids and for marriage are common characteristics of Yanomama village life. With small-number volatility added to these characteristics, it is difficult to see where assumptions of stability lead to fruitful analysis of population dynamics.

Figure 10.4 graphs the age schedules of mortality for each phase of this study and compares them with the average for all three. (The average curve for all phases is the same in Fig. 10.3 and 10.4.) The different shapes and levels of the curves for each phase in Fig. 10.4 show the difficulty, if not futility, of seeking general levels for the demographic variables of this type of population when attempting an analysis of their population dynamics. This indicates the invalidity of abstracting from the essential dynamics of their small size and differing social–biological conditions.

C. Preferential Female Infanticide

Why were the high mortality levels of the models accepted as reasonable for the Yanomamo? They were seen as correcting for known deficiencies of an unknown magnitude in the field data and supplying estimates where no data existed. In addition they were seen by MacCluer *et al.* and Neel-Weiss as confirmation of Chagnon's earlier position on preferential female infanticide. Chagnon realized the weakness of his data on infants and infanticides. He found in his data a high sex ratio at birth of 140. Employing from conventional demography the rule of thumb of a 105 sex ratio at birth, he conjectured large omission of female infanticides and consequently a high infant mortality rate from this and other causes. The high infant mortality given by the models was seen as confirmation and the figures adjusted for the sex preference. However the use of the 105 sex ratio by conventional demography is a norm for large-scale societies and ignores the volatility in anthropological populations. By itself it cannot be used to estimate the magnitude of female infanticide. Chagnon also claimed that female infants were deliberately neglected so that they would die, leading to elevated child mortality.

Other ethnographers denied the importance of preferential female infanticide. Smole (1976) had noted that there was not a high incidence of it in the Parima Highland area. Lizot (1977, 1985) said the literature had exaggerated its incidence. He also denied any deliberate neglect of female babies. Valero (Cocco, 1972) said there was little infanticide for any reason among the groups with whom she lived, which included people in Chagnon's database. As the evidence mounted, Chagnon (Chagnon *et al.*, 1979) rejected his previous position about the importance of preferential female infanticide. Melancon did not work with the assumption of high preferential female infanticide and saw underenumeration as the more important factor for the reported sex ratios.

D. The "Sex Ratio Problem" of the Yanomama

Chagnon (1977) originally held that the Yanomamo populations had more males than females due to preferential female infanticide and this was the main cause of conflict. If the amount of preferential female infanticide has been exaggerated, are the sex ratios of Yanomama populations still female deficient?

Several clarifications are needed. Female infanticide primarily affects the sex ratio at birth, which is distinct from the sex ratio of the
total population. The latter is affected by the additional factors entering into differential mortality and out-migration. Therefore even if a
Yanomama population has a dominant male sex ratio, it cannot be
concluded that there is high preferential female infanticide. Also the
unit of analysis needs to be distinguished. Is the discussion about a
large subgroup of Yanomama or an individual village, which is the
basic unit of dynamics? When Chagnon *et al.* (1979) pooled his data
from 13 villages, he found a sex ratio of 118. When the individual
village is taken as the unit of analysis, there is male dominance, but
it is not overwhelming. This is shown in Table 10.2, which has been
compiled from the literature with data on 21 villages (one at three
different times) in the south central and southwestern sectors. There
is male dominance in 13 villages, but there is female dominance in 8,
and 2 are equal. The Mucajai data show a changing sex ratio over the
28 years. The sex ratio for the combined 17 villages with quantitative
data is 109, which is not an unusual ratio. These data show that not
only has the incidence of female infanticide been exaggerated, but so
has the extent of male-dominated sex ratios of the population at the
village level.

Lizot (1984) gives a striking example of the impact of small-number
volatility on the sex ratio. Table 10.2 shows his enumeration of the
Narimibiwei group with a sex ratio of 122, indicating male dominance. Later this group fissioned into two villages. One of the resulting villages changed to a dominant female sex ratio due to a slight
excess of women, while the other village had a large deficit of females.

The broader question which stimulated the sex-ratio discussion remains. Is there a shortage of females who are both acceptable and
available as sexual partners for Yanomama men? Even if there are
balanced sex ratios of the population, there is a shortage. An important reason is the cultural prescription of postpartum restraint while
the nursling is still at the breast. This lasts for about 3 years, although
both this study and Chagnon have noted that it is not always followed
for the entire period. Another reason is the taking of wives by older
men, either as additional wives or after discarding older wives when
they reach menopause. In addition, there is the problem of enough
females with proper kin relationship to the males. Therefore the ques-

Table 10.2
Male or Female Dominance of 21 Villages in South
Central and Southwestern Yanomama Regions[a]

Village	Male		Female
Upper Biassi-teri	37	<	48
Lower Biassi-teri	25	<	26
Monou-teri	34	>	32
Reyabobowei-teri	52	>	46
Momaribowei-teri	50	>	46
Patanowa-teri	122	>	90
Aikam-teri and Roko-teri	129	>	103
Iyewei-teri (Santa Maria)	53	>	51
Witokaya-teri (Lechosa)	50	<	64
Karoh-teri, 1970	26	=	26
Karoh-teri, 1972	23	<	25
Karoh-teri, after 1972	31	=	31
Kakashiwe	19	>	16
Ihirubiteri	30	>	21
Niyayoba Shabono	102	<	108
Niyayoba-teri	28	<	30
Jorocoba-teri	37	>	36
Narimibiwei	61	>	50
Yebiyobe	38	>	24
Namowei-teri	—	>	—
Xipariwei-teri	—	>	—
Shama-teri	—	<	—
Puunabiwei-teri	—	<	—
Total	898		822
	Sex ratio = 109		
	13 male dominant		8 female dominant

[a]Sources: Chagnon (1977); Cocco (1972); Lizot (1977, 1984); Smole (1976).

tion of a shortage of female sexual partners is much broader than that of the sex ratio, either at birth or of the population.

VI. Stationary or Increasing Population?

The Mucajai data show that the population is increasing, although at a wide variety of rates. Is this the pattern in the other areas or are the Yanomama a stationary population as anthropologists have tradition-ally characterized such populations? This question is confused in the literature by the lack of distinctions about the unit of analysis and the time frame. Is the discussion about individual villages or a bloc of them? Is it a short-run or long-run consideration?

Lizot (1971, 1977) says the Yanomamo were an increasing population. This statement applies to a large population bloc in the long run and for precontact conditions. In the postcontact condition he sees them as undergoing population decrease because the mortality from infectious disease is outstripping fertility.

Smole (1976), in spite of the high rate of group increase given by his crude rates, holds that the Yanomama were traditionally a stationary population. This stability came from an unspecified moderate fertility rate due to the spacing techniques of lactation, abortion, and infanticide, which were offset by an unspecified moderate mortality level without any notable health problems. He sees the use of lactation, abortion, and infanticide as means to tailor their population size to the availability of their resources and this as the reason they are not a high-fertility population. He recognizes later changes but does not discuss their demographic structure.

Neel and Weiss (1975) consider their use of stable models to estimate Yanomamo demographic values as successful and see this as confirmation that the Yanomama are close to being stable populations. Neel (1969) earlier saw stability indicated by Chagnon's 3.8 total fertility rate and maintained by "their apparent commitment to population control and their efforts to live in harmony with their ecosystem." Later, when the models produced very high mortality, stability was achieved by postulating very high group fertility.

The study of the Mucajai group has shown a different set of reasons for the use of lactation, abortion, and infanticide. They do result in spacing, but not enough to bring the number of live births below seven to eight, which many would still characterize as high fertility. But the reasons indicated in Chapter 4 for lactation and Chapter 7 for abortion and infanticide have nothing to do with a deliberate effort to limit the overall number of births. The use of the semantic "population control" for this type of fertility regime is, at best, a loose use of words and, at worst, an ethnocentric distortion from a different type of social system with its distinctive fertility regime. Preferential female infanticide is practiced precisely to hasten another pregnancy and birth, hopefully a male. It is not done simply to remove a female from the population. Cocco (1972) also notes this important point for the Yanomamo area. This is not the strategy of people exercising population control for the sake of holding down the overall number of offspring. The same logic lies behind an abortion or infanticide to protect the nursling at the breast. If lowering the number of surviving offspring were the goal of the behavior, why bother to protect the nursling? A similar logic is behind abortion when a girl is considered too young to become a mother. If holding down numbers is the object of the strategy, why protect future pregnancies and births? This is not population control in the ordinary sense of this semantic. These practices must be interpreted against their distinctive cultural background.

In conclusion, the Mucajai research appears applicable to other Yanomama groups and allows some generalization. Fertility patterns and their demographic levels appear almost universal in the region. Neither preferential female infanticide nor infanticide for any reason are extensively practiced. There is great volatility in all Yanomama demographic rates because of the small numbers. Consequently no demographic norms from large-scale societies can be used by themselves to interpret Yanomama demographic data. The sex ratio at birth has high variance for this reason, but not because of widespread female infanticide. The total fertility rate is between seven and eight, making the Yanomama a relatively high-fertility population. They cannot be characterized as a low-fertility population as implied by the early 3.8 total fertility rate. The use of extended lactation, abortion, and infanticide is consistent with this relatively high fertility level. An important reason for their use is to help living people survive, or to hasten additional births. They are not practiced to limit the size of the population for any reason including adjustment to available resources.

The patterns of migration are typical. There are no data with which to compare their demographic levels.

The causes of death appear typical. The lesser intensity of warfare in the southeastern and south central regions will probably yield lower mortality levels than those of the southwestern area. While the Yanomamo can have periods of high mortality, especially when suffering from epidemics of infectious disease, they are not a continually high-mortality population.

VII. Some Implications for Population Research on Small-Scale Anthropological Societies

This investigation has employed a database rich in demographic and ethnographic detail. This is unusual since most studies of anthropological populations have used only fragmentary information. It has yielded insights into the population dynamics and problems of analysis which appear to have wider application to other small-scale anthropological populations.

The traditional view has been that these societies approximate the model of a stationary population. Weiss (1973), repeating this consensus, has observed: "In general, the assumptions of a stationary population are reasonable. . . . Most anthropological populations are observed under nearly stable conditions, . . . for they generally represent precontact conditions when cultural change was presumably slower." Although this study has concentrated on the immediate postcontact period, it questions the assumption of stationarity as meaningful for the analysis of the population dynamics for groups such as the Yanomama.

A. Fertility

The age at menarche helps determine the length of the reproductive span. The average age for Mucajai girls is 12.4 years. This average age is comparable with the averages for industrial countries. Given the description in Chapter 1 of the foods available to the Mucajai through horticulture, hunting, gathering, and fishing as well as the evidence from nutritional studies of other Yanomama (Chagnon and Hames, 1979), the Yanomama are well nourished populations. This provides support for the hypothesis that early age at menarche is correlated with good nutrition, whatever specific mechanisms may be involved (Frisch 1975, 1984).

Average individual fertility is high, around eight live births per female. Cohabitation begins young, but adolescent sterility may be operative in postponing the average age of the mother at the first child to 16.8 years. Induced abortion also has a role in this delay. Nursing and induced abortion after the contraceptive effect of lactation ends extend the birth intervals. This is done solely to protect the nursling and without concern for the number of children or availability of resources beyond the mother's milk. Protection of the nursling emerges from this study as the key motivation for spacing. The contraceptive effect of lactation contributes to this protection even though it is not fully realized by Yanomama women. The research has shown high fertility with considerable child survival is compatible with the usage of induced abortion and infanticide.

The analysis has also shown the necessity of distinguishing individual from group fertility in such populations. To state that these are high-fertility populations refers only to the fertility of individual women. This cannot be projected automatically to group fertility because the relationship can vary depending on the age–sex composition of the population. Annual crude rates are highly volatile because of the small number of the births and potential volatility of the age–sex structure. Over the long run there is no evidence that this volatility subsides to any stable average. Even if long-run stability occurs, it definitely cannot be interpolated to shorter time intervals that provide most research on this topic.

This research has also shown the logical possibility of combining high individual fertility and low group fertility through a low sex ratio. It raises the possibility that some populations who are facing a shortage of necessary resources might deliberately attempt to use the sex ratio as a means of group fertility control in spite of high rates of total fertility.

B. Migration

The conventional assumption of demographic stability requires a population closed to migration. An exact interpretation of the assumption means long-term closure, which does not eliminate short-term migration as long as it balances out in the long term both in total numbers and in age–sex composition. In practice, however, the stability assumption has meant a tendency to ignore migration even in the short run. Methodologically migration is usually a difficult variable to study. In spite of this problem, this research has shown its strategic importance in the population dynamics of the Yanomama. Since the Yanomama practices of fission, intervillage marriage, and taking captives are present in many foraging/horticultural societies, migration cannot be ignored in the studies of this type of society.

The frequent neglect of migration raises the issue of the levels of analysis, which also affects all the other demographic variables. The village or a group of interactive villages is the level of analysis required to understand population dynamics. Larger levels of aggregation may be used, such as a large population bloc or the whole group specified by some generic name. These larger abstractions may offer methodological or conceptual advantages. It may be possible to assume absence of migration in spite of large intralevel migration. Small-number volatility may be mitigated by pooling of data. But whether these are useful analytical advantages depends on the question being investigated. The literature is weak on specifying the levels of analysis, perhaps on the fallacious assumption that the analysis of one level can be extrapolated automatically to the next. Patterns of migration among the Mucajai clearly demonstrate the fallacy. The assumption of stationarity may have some validity at some very high level of aggregation, but if this is the only information available, it tells nothing about the population dynamics of the constituent groups. One may speculate that, in the early history of man, villages were continually going out of existence as they were overwhelmed by demographic loss from mortality or out-migration or lowered fertility due to volatile sex ratios. These forces could also be combined. On the other hand, other villages may have been going through population explosions because of the reverse of these factors. Perhaps at some very high level of aggregation the population of the expanding villages equaled those of the disappearing villages, giving the assumption of stationarity some basis.

VIII. The Evolution of Human Population Dynamics

The contemporary world is in the process of cultural and demographic evolution. This evolution is complicated by the fact that the contemporary world is a mixture of several types of human societies representing various stages of cultural evolution. Because one aspect of contemporary evolution involves the popularly called "population explosion" of agricultural societies, much effort has been expended to understand and cope with it. "Demographic transition theory" has been the intellectual basis for much of these efforts in spite of serious deficiencies with the theory, especially with regard to explaining high fertility and the change to low fertility. The present study provides a picture of a fertility structure which preceded the contemporary fertility structures of agricultural societies, thereby providing a comparative basis to begin to understand the evolutionary process. The fertility structure presented in this study was not affected by contact and appears to represent a very old regime of fertility. It shows that the high-fertility structures are not tied to high-mortality structures as argued by some. There was deliberate spacing of births with protection of the nursling the primary reason. The spacing provided by lactation is shown to be important, but was supplemented by other methods and was subordinate to protection of the nursling rather than an effort to limit the size of the population. The Mucajai data also suggest that high infant, child, and maternal mortality are not characteristics of foraging/horticultural societies and perhaps do not become systemic characteristics until the emergence of large-scale agricultural societies.

IX. Conclusion

The primary efforts of this research have been to understand the population dynamics of the Mucajai Yanomama. The investigators believe that they have collected and analyzed the most complete and accurate data on a foraging/horticultural group to date. These data have allowed questions to be raised that can only be answered by further studies. This research has also contributed to a better understanding of the substantive and methodological problems of investigating population dynamics in other small-scale anthropological populations. Only by understanding the population dynamics of these societies can we begin to understand the evolution to the dynamics of large-scale peasant and industrial societies, in other words, to help understand ourselves.

References

Anderson, P.
1983. *Curr. Anthropol.* **24,** 25–45.

Bongaarts, J., and Potter, R. G.
1983. "Fertility, Biology and Behavior." Academic Press, New York.

Chagnon, N.
1968. *In* "War: The Anthropology of Armed Conflict and Aggression" (M. Fried, M. Harris, and R. Murphy, eds.), pp. 109–159. Natural History Press, New York.

Chagnon, N.
1972. *In* "The Structure of Human Populations" (G. A. Harrison and A. J. Boyce, eds.), pp. 252–282. Clarendon Press, Oxford.

Chagnon, N.
1974. "Studying the Yanomamo." Holt, Rinehart & Winston, New York.

Chagnon, N.
1977. "Yanomamo: The Fierce People" 2nd ed. Holt, Rinehart & Winston, New York.

Chagnon, N.
1983. "Yanomamo: The Fierce People" 3rd ed. Holt, Rinehart & Winston, New York.

Chagnon, N.
1988. *Science* **239,** 985–992.

Chagnon, N. A., and Hames, R. B.
1979. *Science* **203,** 910–913.

Chagnon, N. A., Neel, J. V., Weitkamp, L., Gershowitz, H., and Ayres, M.
1970. *Am. J. Phys. Anthropol.* **32,** 339–349.

Chagnon, N., Flinn, M., and Melancon, T.
1979. *In* "Evolutionary Biology and Human Social Behavior" (N. Chagnon and W. Irons, eds.), pp. 290–320. Duxbury Press, North Scituate, Massachusetts.

Coale, A. J., and Demeny, P.
1966. "Regional Model Life Tables and Stable Populations." Princeton University Press, Princeton, New Jersey.

Cocco, L.
1972. "Iyewei-Teri: Quince Años Entre los Yanomamos." Escuela Tecnica Popular Don Bosco, Caracas.

Colchester, M.
1982. *Antropologica* **57,** 91–95.

Colchester, M.
1985. *In* "The Health and Survival of the Venezuelan Yanoama" (M. Colchester, ed.), pp. 1–11. The International Work Group for Indigenous Affairs, Document 53, Copenhagen.

Early, J. D.
1982. "The Demographic Structure and Evolution of a Peasant System: The Guatemalan Population." University Presses of Florida, Boca Raton, Florida.

Early, J. D.
1985. *Hum. Biol.* **57,** 387–399.

Frisch, R. E.
1975. *Social Biol.* **22,** 17–22.

Frisch, R. E.
1984. *Biol. Rev.* **59,** 161–188.

Gregor, T.
1985. "Anxious Pleasures: The Sexual Lives of an Amazonian People." University of Chicago Press, Chicago.

Konner, M., and Worthman, C.
1980. *Science* **207,** 788–791.

Lizot, J.
1971. *J. Societe de Americanistes* **60,** 137–175.

Lizot, J.
1975. *"El Hombre de la Pantorrilla Prenada,"* Monografia No. 21. Fundación la Salle de Ciencas Naturales, Caracas.

Lizot, J.
1977. *Man* **12,** 497–517.

Lizot, J.

1984. "Les Yanomami Centraux." Editions de L'Ecole des Hautes Etudes en Sciences Sociales, Paris.

Lizot, J.

1985. "Tales of the Yanomami." Cambridge University Press, Cambridge, Massachusetts.

Lizot, J.

1988. "Los Yanomami," In *Los Aborigenes de Venezuela* (W. Coppens, ed.), Volumen III, Etnologia Contemporanea II (J. Lizot, ed.) pp. 479–583, Monografia No. 35. Fundación la Salle de Ciencas Naturales, Caracas.

MacCluer, J. W., Neel, J. V., and Chagnon, N. A.

1971. *Am. J. Phys. Anthropol.* **35,** 193–207.

Melancon, T. F.

1982. "Marriage and Reproduction among the Yanomamo Indians of Venezuela." Doctoral Dissertation, The Pennsylvania State University. University Microfilms International, #8213331, Ann Arbor, Michigan.

Melatti, J. C.

1979. *In* "Dialectical Societies: The Ge and Bororo of Central Brazil" (D. Maybury-Lewis, ed.), pp. 46–79. Harvard University Press, Cambridge, Massachusetts.

Migliazza, E. C.

1964. *Boletim Do Museu Paraense Emilio Goeldi* **22,** 1–19.

Migliazza, E. C.

1980. *Antropologica* **53,** 95–162.

Migliazza, E. C.

1982. *In* "Biological Diversification in the Tropics" (G. T. Prance, ed.), pp, 497–519. Columbia University Press, New York.

Murphy, Y., and Murphy, R.

1974. "Women of the Forest." Columbia University Press, New York.

Neel, J. V.

1969. *Proc. 12th Int. Cong. Genet.* **3,** 389–403.

Neel, J. V., and Chagnon, N. A.

1968. *Proc. Natl. Acad. Sci. U.S.A.* **59,** 680–689.

Neel, J. V., and Weiss, K.

1975. *Am. J. Phys. Anthropol.* **42,** 25–51.

Peters, J. F.

1974. *Social Biol.* **21,** 58–69.

Peters, J. F.
1980. *Social Biol.* **27,** 272–285.

Peters, J. F.
1982. *J. Comp. Fam. Stud.* **13,** 87–95.

Peters, J. F.
1984. *J. Comp. Fam. Stud.* **15,** 151–174.

Peters, J. F.
1987. *J. Comp. Fam. Stud.* **18,** 79–98.

Peters, J. F, and Hunt, C.
1975. J. Comp. Fam. Stud. **6,** 197–207.

Short, R. V.
1984. *Scientific Am.* 252, 35–41.

Smole, W. J.
1976. "The Yanoama Indians—A Cultural Geography." University of Texas Press, Austin.

Steinvorth Goetz, I.
1969. "Uriji Jami!" Asociación Cultural Humboldt, Caracas.

Valero, H.
1984. *"Yo Soy Napeyoma,"* Mongrafia No. 35. Fundación La Salle de Ciencias Naturales, Caracas.

Wagley, C.
1977. "Welcome of Tears." Oxford University Press, New York.

Weiss, K.
1973. *"American Antiquity,"* Vol. 38., No. 2, Part II. Society for American Archeology, Memoirs No. 27.

Index

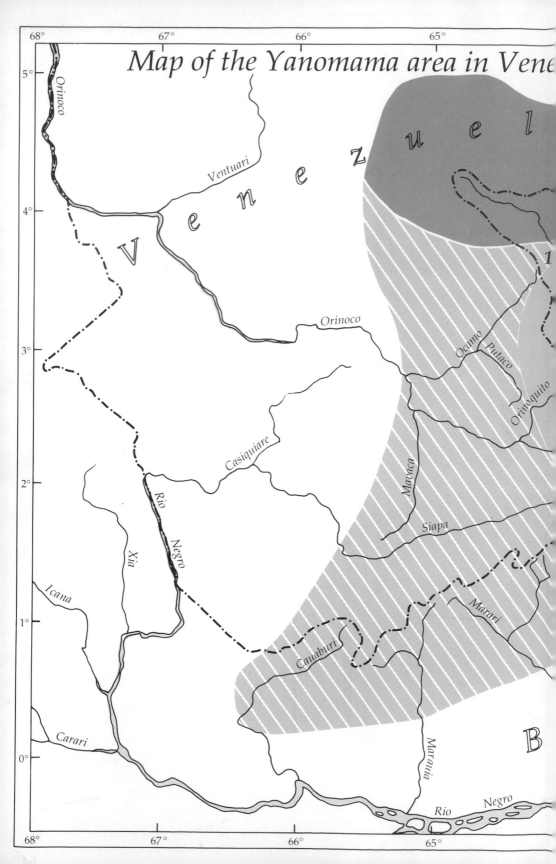